W. James Seymour

The opinions expressed in this manuscript are solely the opinions of the author and do not represent the opinions or thoughts of the publisher. The author has represented and warranted full ownership and/or legal right to publish all the materials in this book.

In the Jungle...
Camping with the Enemy
All Rights Reserved.
Copyright © 2014 W. James Seymour
v2.0

Cover Image by W. James Seymour

This book may not be reproduced, transmitted, or stored in whole or in part by any means, including graphic, electronic, or mechanical without the express written consent of the publisher except in the case of brief quotations embodied in critical articles and reviews.

Outskirts Press, Inc.
http://www.outskirtspress.com

ISBN: 978-1-4787-2983-9

Outskirts Press and the "OP" logo are trademarks belonging to Outskirts Press, Inc.

PRINTED IN THE UNITED STATES OF AMERICA

To all Viet-Nam veterans who might read this book:

We all have stories. Some we've told, some we have not. Some we for- got; some we tried to forget.

As in the seemingly differing reports of the three blind men describing the elephant… these are MY personal memories; these vivid, excitable memories of a 20 year-old youth, yet composed in the calm detached manner of a comfortable middle-aged man.

This book is therefore dedicated to all of our families and friends – the ones who have put up with us since our return!

TO ALL OF THE LRRPS and RANGERS OF MY WAR….

Were it not for this unique conflict,

Were it not for the U. S. Army,

And without the draft,

I never would have rubbed shoulders with you guys!

You are men worth knowing… and I am proud to have met you!

Spanky

# Contents

# Acknowledgments

Special thanks to Bruce Judkins for letting me read some of his letters home and pages from his journal. This was instrumental in keeping the facts and their sequences straight on several missions mentioned in the narrative.

And I extend a heartfelt thank-you and gratitude to my ex-teammate Tom Chambers. After a many-year delayed phone conversation, the idea of stringing these stories together was generated – hence the book!

And to the 'literate LLRP' of my unit, Kregg Jorgenson: Thanks for taking the point and guiding me through both the book creation and book publishing jungles. This book would not have existed without your assistance.

# Prologue

I looked again at my watch and read 4:10 on the luminous dial. Another 20 minutes and I would awaken the other four members of my LRRP team, Slashing Talon 32 – or, for the sake of brevity, just '3-2' on the radio.

BMNT was at 4:45 that day. That's Beginning Morning Nautical Twilight, commonly called the 'false dawn.' Actual sunrise that particular morning would not occur until 5:07, but at BMNT the advance light of the approaching sun would gradually lighten the night's darkness until the sun's disc would break over the eastern horizon at precisely 5:07, the official beginning of the day. The significance of the false dawn to us was that we could then distinguish individual silhouettes from the jungle shadows.

Up to this point it had been a quiet and uneventful reconnaissance, now the third day of a five day mission. We had been assigned an area approximately ten kilometers from the Cambodian border, an area from which the NVA 9th Regiment was either staging from, or else using as an access route into Tay Ninh Province. So far we had heard and seen nothing.

I looked at my sleeping teammates and smiled inwardly, a smile of fond satisfaction. This was a good team, one that I felt confident and safe with. There was SP/4 Tom Chambers, a large 6'4" black hulk who

I'd designated as team medic – not for his medical expertise, since we were all equally trained in first aid and battle-field repair, but simply because he was large enough to carry the unwieldy medic kit with a minimum of effort and inconvenience. His weapon of choice was an old grease-gun, or 'burp' gun, of WW2 paratrooper fame. He was also big enough to handle the weight of 20 spare magazines of heavy .45 caliber rounds.

My assistant team-leader was SGT Mike Carrol, who'd been with me for four missions now. We worked well together and I did not have to oversee his duties and responsibilities – they got done, whatever they were. He was previously a bank teller from someplace in New England and he had the unique ability of always looking fresh and dapper. It was downright uncanny, for he never appeared dirty, even after spending several days in the bush.

The other two men were fairly new, this being their second mission each, but they were performing well and learning the ropes admirably. Their roles were those of RTO and rear-scout/security. I had no misgivings about either of them fitting into the team.

My reverie over, I leaned to my left and nudged Carrol awake, then did the same to the RTO on my right. They in turn woke the others. In our classic star position for the night we had simply arranged our packs in a tight circle with our bodies and legs extending outwards in all directions. In this arrangement our heads were close enough to talk low with each other, yet observe outwards in all directions around our position.

Once awake we remained in our positions, our packs propping us as our pillows, and listened while the jungle woke up as the darkness diminished. The vegetation had a dry yellow color due to the lack of moisture, yet this dryness mandated a noisy crispy rustling sound as it was disturbed. That is what we were listening for – any movement at all around us would let us know that we were not alone.

It was our habit, learned from past experiences, to lay and listen for approximately 20 minutes, making sure that we were alone before we would even think of moving ourselves, and then the preparation of our morning coffee or cocoa and a light breakfast would begin. We would also call in our morning situation report to our home base to let the rear HQ's know our status prior to moving from our night's location.

As I was about to heat some water for my coffee, leaves rustled to my direct front about 20 meters distant. I slid my CAR-15 across my lap and alerted the man to my right, pointing to my front as I did so. He in turn grabbed his weapon and alerted the next man. Looking over my left shoulder I could see Carrol's rifle pointing to the sound – he had heard it too.

All of us ready now, we waited and listened as the rustling drew closer, straight towards us. Directly to me. My weapon was pointed to my front, between my legs, as I reclined against my pack.

Ten meters now, it sounded like, getting closer. Deliberate movement, in a straight line. Right to us.

Five meters. Inside our claymores now, but still unseen.

I heard the sound, behind me, of a safety selector being released. I would have to remember to mention this to the RTO, still learning, afterwards. "Keep your weapon *always* ready to fire in the woods. The 'safe' setting is for back in the rear only."

About 10 feet in front of me now – should be able to see them any second. Taking a breath, I lay still, stock still, and dug my heels in, anticipating the rifle's recoil when fired.

Here they are, I thought, as I could now see the bushy branches move.

Suddenly I froze in slack-jawed amazement and disbelief as a huge ***tiger's head,*** as large as my pack, poked through the branches not 8 feet away! Laying as I was, I was looking slightly upwards as the beast broke through the foliage, its coloring blending perfectly with the shadows of the early morning light.

The animal took two steps before it sensed, or saw us, and with a start it snorted a deep 'chuff,' then sprang directly at/over me (and our position) and landed six feet past on the other side and sped off without a sound.

Craning my head around to see where it went, I saw Chambers

staring incredulously, mouth agape. It had happened so fast that none of us even thought of firing. He returned my questioning look with a shake of his head and a wan smile.

"Not only is this crazy war unreal" I muttered, reaching again for my coffee-makings, "but we're fighting in a goddamn zoo!"

# Chapter One

"Which school are you going to next year?"

In my senior year of high school, 1964-65, this was ***the question,*** heard everywhere – in the hallways, in the cafeteria, in the study halls, locker rooms, and parking lot – virtually everywhere that a conversation occurred.

It was also the question that I most dreaded. Instead of replying with a college's initial or name, like the U of W or Seattle University, I would answer "None, next year. My folks can't afford the tuition so I'll work for a year to save up." My grades were definitely good enough for college entrance and I even sent out a couple of half-hearted admission applications. But in the back of my mind I knew that I couldn't save up four year's college tuition in that amount of time, straight out of high school.

For me high school had been fun. All of my friends were there, it was the social hub of every teenager's existence in that era and besides, it got me out of the house! I enjoyed my classes and I was athletic (or so I thought), having turned out for every sport in season since the eighth grade.

Coming from a blue-collar family and mostly raised by a working single mother it was fascinating for me to hear adults (teachers and coaches) talk knowledgeably about topics that were never brought up in family talks: i.e., the impact of the printing press, the after-effects of the French Revolution, the new astronomical discovery labeled a 'quasar' and the very idea that the recently developed electron microscope could take a picture of an organic cell's nucleus, amid all that cytoplasm! This was not the stuff of dinner conversations at home, mostly eaten off of T.V. trays in the living room in front of the television set.

Up to now school had been an exhilarating and pre-dominant force in my life. My role, my purpose, *my job*, as a kid was that of a student. Now I'm going to graduate, a large milestone was to be passed. But then what? What do I do? What can I do?

As I was growing up I used to listen in wide-eyed fascination at family get-togethers, as the men would recount their military experiences. This uncle was in the army, that one was in the navy; my father was in the navy and later my stepfather was in the marines. Listening to them I got the impression that it was almost expected of me as a matter of course to eventually join one of the service branches to mature, in order to become one of them, an adult male member in good family standing.

I wanted to be a paratrooper, to jump out of airplanes and do heroic deeds with my fellow soldiers. This was my secret fantasy persona, my childish view of a man in uniform that I'd held inside my head ever since I started watching war movies, or sitting in front of the TV in the evening at family time mesmerized by the popular series 'Victory at Sea.' I really liked the music of the shows, but in retrospect I think they served more as subliminal recruiting programs than as wholesome television fare.

I enjoyed the summer of '65. I water-skied four times a week with a new friend, had my first girlfriend (girls were different, thought differently, and I didn't understand them at all!) and got my first car, a '53 Chevrolet station wagon that was taller than I was.As the summer wore on and fall approached I began to realize that I was in the same place as earlier: a directionless young kid, school's over, no real plan, and no money in the bank.

I started picking up military recruiting pamphlets at the Post Office from all of the services. I didn't want to talk to a recruiter yet, but I was interested. I began recalling all of the military conversations at past family functions. And I started watching the TV news and reading the newspapers, *really* reading the newspapers. Something was beginning to flare up in Asia in a little-known place called Viet Nam, wherever the heck that was.

I remembered seeing a movie on television with my grandfather about World War 1, titled "Paths of Glory" starring Kirk Douglas, recently of "Spartacus" fame. The movie depicted a disastrous French infantry attack on a well-fortified German position and illustrated trench warfare at its worst.

My grandfather did not serve in WW1 (he had a shipyard job) but a lot of his friends did and he always told their stories. Right after the horrible massacre on the screen he looked at me and said "If you ever go into the service, try to get into a small unit if you can. Those men were used as cannon-fodder and only luck, not training or ability, decided who would survive." Then he launched into another of his friends' war stories. But his words of warning stuck with me.

As my collection of recruiting pamphlets grew, something new being offered by the Army caught my interest. A new organization called the Special Forces, composed primarily of 12-man A-Teams, seemed to offer the specialized training yet retain a sense of individuality that appealed to me. They were comprised of two officers and ten soldiers specializing in weapons, demolitions, communications and medical expertise, yet cross-trained in all other fields so they could fill in if a team-member was absent. To an idealistic youth as I this was perfect, yet what did I know of any of these fields?

A hesitant conversation with an Army Recruiter solidified my concerns – I had to be 21 years of age to qualify. But, and here was the catch, the Army would allow me to attend the Airborne Jump School and train me in radio communications to gain some experience prior to joining the SF, as he called it. Plus, with this minor brush-war in Viet Nam heating up it looked like I might have some experience in a combat zone behind me to further my chances for acceptance. Knowing from nothing as I did, this sounded good to me.

Besides, I really liked the idea that these guys were usually operating in god-forsaken areas, not really with the army at all, living with the local inhabitants far from the beaten path. The fact that these teams were expected to live off the land, on their own initiative and ingenuity did not detract from the romantic image, either. This sounded like a grand adventure with a capital A!

So I enlisted. I took a series of tests as part of the paperwork game – this one for intelligence, that one for compatibility, and the important one (to my plans anyhow) for communications aptitude. I thought it an easy one really, sort of a primer for Morse code training. Anyhow, my test results guaranteed that the Army would train me in everything that I asked for. All I had to do was do my best. To a high-school athlete it sounded very much like business as usual – 'train hard and learn.'

A bonus was that I did not have to go in right away – my reporting date was the day after Thanksgiving, giving me plenty of time to visit with friends and family before the military phase of my life would begin.

I was sent to Fort Ord, California for my basic training and had a good time. In my 48-man training platoon we were all volunteers except for two, who had volunteered for the draft. As a result our spirits were high and we were all motivated. No one fought the system and we all got along. It was also my introduction to lack of reason of 'the Army way' for about two thirds of the platoon was from the Pacific Northwest yet we were sent all the way to California instead of being trained at Ft. Lewis in Washington. Also we learned that the Beach Boys and all the surfer-songs had lied to us, for we froze our butts in sunny Monterey!

It was at Fort Ord's in-processing center, during the day-long battery of psychological and aptitude testing to determine our individual interests, abilities, intelligence, and personal talents, that I had passed with flying colors the Army's Officer Candidate Examination, indicating I had the requisite smarts to be an officer. In the first week of basic training the fourteen of us in the company that had passed were encouraged to apply for OCS (Officer Candidate School), both for our personal benefit and the needs of the service. Knowing from nothing, it sounded good to us, so we all signed up for it.

But as basic training progressed I began to understand that military service was a lot more complex and sophisticated than the simplistic view that I had received from the movies and second-hand conversations. I realized that I knew nothing about service life, and really could not picture myself as a Second Lieutenant, giving orders, for example, to my drill sergeant! And so, in the sixth week of basic training I withdrew my OCS application, citing lack of experience, and felt that I was back on track as to my original plan.

After basic training was completed the Army kept me at Ft. Ord for radio training for an additional ten weeks. The in-service nickname for this course was the "ditty-dumdum-ditty" school, in reference to the international Q and Z signal of IMI overscored, that is, the Morse characters I, M and I again, sent together with no break in between letters, a shorthand notation meaning 'say again." The first three weeks were nerve-wracking, listening to Morse code's dit-dah for at least seven hours a day. It seemed that every week an average of two personnel would rip off their headsets in frustration and quit the school. It was common knowledge that these drop-outs would be re-assigned to infantry training and that was enough to keep the rest of us motivated – for didn't our test scores alone prove to the Army that we were more than just infantry candidates?

But towards the end, after the weeding-out process took its toll, it became interesting and a semblance of relevancy settled in. For this was when we were taught the ins and outs of various field radios, their installation and operation, and how to load them using both standard and field-expedient (improvised) antennas. Then in the last week we were sent in teams to various locations throughout Ft. Ord to set up and operate radio communication nets, utilizing all that we had learned. Many guys here were also excited for if they did well enough in training they would qualify for their amateur radio operator's (ham radio) license. To me it was simply a necessary step towards my personal goal, but nevertheless I was glad when the course was over and we graduated.

It was during this radio operator's course that I developed a strong friendship with a fellow student, Larry Newport. We had a lot in common – we were both jump school volunteers, we both had a high-school athletic background, we had the same barracks, and we both expected to graduate on the same day, then go to Ft. Benning together. We just seemed to hit it off well together, as friendships inexplicably do.

But two days before our Friday graduation Larry got orders to depart early for jump school, and I didn't get any at all. It seems that my original OCS application had taken me off jump school orders and the Army had re-directed me as an A.I. (Assistant Instructor) in a basic training unit here at Ft. Ord. The rationale here was that all OCS applicants would benefit greatly from the leadership experiences involved with AI duty, and would attend jump school after graduation from OCS.

I was really pleased for Larry's sake, and his enthusiasm and excitement were contagious – but I was also kind of sad for me. Apparently the withdrawal of my OCS application required more time delay for the Army personnel offices to get me back on orders for a jump-school class starting date, and I would have to pull about a month of AI duty, regardless.

Larry left early Friday morning with a couple of others, for the airport. We traded addresses and vowed to stay in touch. He would miss radio-school graduation, but he would arrive at jump-school in Ft. Benning, Ga. after midnight, with his class starting on Monday. Perfect!

Larry's plane was a small private charter service, under contract, carrying about 65 soldiers to Georgia. That evening it crashed, in bad weather, in the mountains of Arkansas.

There were no survivors.

*An athlete's grin, a sardonic smile*
*Plus a cynical look that made it worthwhile*
*To fathom the meanings of a brain*
*That shall never reason again.*
*A loner, as I, yet not so extrovert*
*As to leave one feeling hurt*
*Because he wants not to talk –*
*Would rather meditate, then go for a walk.*
*A loner not really, but then just a little*
*Since he stated he hates to be caught in the middle.*
*But when you know him, a friendship ensues:*
*Not in threes, but rather in twos.*
*A determined air, and a definite purpose*
*Had set him on one course –*
*A Green Beret, above the rest;*
*Confident, since he had passed the test.*
*We were like brothers in various ways*
*Even to the counting of our days.*
*I'll miss him, that much I know;*
*And because of him, I'm not afraid to go.*

Eulogy to Larry E. Newport,
Friend and classmate –
Killed in plane crash
April 22, 1966

After a three-week leave at home, the next phase of my military training was the Airborne Jump School at Ft. Benning, Georgia. For this I was very apprehensive, for I had wanted to be paratrooper since I was a little kid and because I wanted it so badly I was nervous. Besides, the army's rumor mill was rife with scare-stories about jump school – the washout rate was as high as 50%, pressure was intense because they didn't want soldiers who couldn't take it, the physical demands were intensely brutal, and the god-like NCO instructors would beat you silly for every mistake you made (remember, this was in the old-army era when physical contact, under the guise of training, was allowed.)

And so, in mid-June of 1966, I reported for in-processing at 2:00 AM on a Saturday morning. The yelling and screaming by the NCOs started right away, before we even disembarked from the buses and in all truthfulness did not stop for the next four weeks. I do remember, during processing, filling out a dream sheet, that is, where do we want to be assigned after graduation? The choices were fairly standard, only locations where airborne units were stationed – Ft. Campbell, Kentucky, Ft. Bragg, North Carolina, Panama, Germany, Okinawa, or Viet Nam. Of course, I opted for Viet Nam – that was part of the plan explained to me by the recruiter and besides, weren't we the good guys that little ol' Viet Nam had asked for help in fending off communist aggression? Didn't all the males in my family at one time serve overseas, setting the example for me to follow? And in all probability, as an airborne radioman, wouldn't I likely be sent there anyhow?

In any event, the next three weeks were like nothing I had ever experienced before in my life.

First off, the instructors tried their damnedest to erase the idea of 'walk' from our heads. We ran, we double-timed, we shuffled, and we sprinted everywhere. The god-awful fear of being late was instilled in us, and wherever we had to go, we HURRIED! If we were in a dogtrot we felt like we were relaxing.

Conversational tones were a thing of the past – everyone yelled and screamed, especially at us students. Even the cooks inside the mess hall. It got to the point that when an instructor yelled in our face so loud and so close that he spit on us we took it as a matter of course, and were no longer shocked. In effect, we learned to tune it out, and began to look back on our basic training Drill Sergeants as beginners.

And I was young and naïve enough to think that I was in shape.

Hah! I was never so exhausted at the end of the day in my life. It seems that we were always doing pushups, either as a punishment, (if one guy in the group screwed up, we all dropped for a minimum of twenty, stood up and yelled 'Thank you, Sergeant.') or even as a reward when the entire group performed well, or at least satisfactorily, for the impossible to please instructors.

And things were different in the airborne. We were all volunteers, highly motivated, but that wasn't enough for many of us. Every day, every hour, it seemed that somebody else threw in the towel and dogtrotted across the training fields to the instructor's shack to quit. Whenever we would see a lone individual heading to that building, the rest of us hardened our resolve.

And terminology was different, too. Our platoons and companies were not composed of squads – they were now called "sticks", for loading into the aircraft and reforming on the drop zones.

And I started to see different people than the age-similar groupings I had been used to all my life. There was a 38 year old Major going through the course with us, there were older personnel from other countries' military qualifying for US jump wings, and people with different attitudes and outlooks than those I was familiar with. I remember that after our fifth and last jump my stick-buddy jokingly remarked that he had now been in an airplane five times, but he still hadn't landed in one – that simple revelation blew my mind!

All in all, I felt ten feet tall when the highly coveted jump wings were pinned to my chest at the graduation ceremony. I truly felt that they were not given to me, but rather that I had earned them. I was proud of them, I'll admit it, but not as a thing for they were cheap – you could buy them in the PX for $.55 – but for what they represented and stood for. But I've always wondered if I'd go through jump school again. Probably not!

We graduated jump school in July, and that afternoon was spent in the barracks area, in formation, while our assignment orders were passed out. Of the 810 who started the class, the attrition due to injury, recycles, and just plain quitting was terrible, for only about 520 graduated as scheduled. This further upped the price of a cheap set of jump wings. And of the 520 who graduated in my class, in July of 1966, 375 at least received orders to report to Viet Nam, after a then-generous 30-day leave. And I was one of them. No real surprise there, for isn't that what I had wanted, to do acts of bravery with my fellow paratroopers?

Next stop - Viet Nam!

### Essay – Attempt at Humor

WHY?

I'm not really sure, but I am nervous – and excited. The fellow across the aisle is talking, I think, since I can see his mouth and jaw in animation but his words are sucked into the background roar, and lost. It is cold, very cold, yet my hands are sweating and my undershirt is sopping. Curiously, my mouth is dry, more so than my worst-ever 'morning after.'

WHY?

The tension is a tangible substance now: it can be felt, it can be smelled – it is here. Uncontrollably, my leg spasms and I lean forward in my seat to put weight on it, to stop the telltale trembling. As I sit back, I look at my buddy of the last month or so and I am startled. I never realized that his eyes were *that* white. I force a grin; he returns it, yet it does not seem right somehow. Curious, that.

I start to daydream, to let my mind wander. No! Be honest now; I am mentally running, seeking solace in something other than the here and now. My buddy and I have endured a lot, have done a lot, and have hurt even more. I know him better than any member of my family, yet he was an unknown just four short weeks ago.

WHY?

Down the aisle perhaps 11 or 12 seats there is sudden movement on my side. I can't see it but somehow I know it. I see shock and surprise in some faces on the other side. As the stench assaults my tenuous hold on self-control, there is no doubt – somebody threw up. I sincerely hope that there is no domino effect.

Surprisingly, I realize that I am tired, very tired. Realization and embarrassment hit at about the same time, and I consciously will my body to relax, to un-tense the muscle groups. It helps, but I still feel tired, wishing it were over.

WHY?

I *know* I am healthy. I *know* I am strong. Lord knows, I've had to prove that in the past four weeks. Brave and courageous? I guess I'll find out. Intelligent? Well…

My left thigh is cramping. The weapons case strapped alongside it prevents me from finding a comfortable position. I try to straighten it and accidentally bump a man across the aisle – not the talker but the fellow sitting next to him, the sleeper (or pray-er, I can't tell). He jolts, eyes now huge, and his complexion pales at a visible rate. I signal 'sorry' to him, and try a helpless grin, but he pivots his head, looks around, and retreats back behind closed eyes.

Strange thoughts, now. All of the old scare stories (unfounded, of course, but often repeated nevertheless) come crowding in under my helmet. What a hell of a time to think about those.

WHY?

A commotion at the door. Two men brutalize it open and the noise is unbearable, yet hypnotic. The throaty drone of the engines is joined by the whine of the wind. And a damn fast wind, at that.

It's time. All of us stand up in the aisle after the usual fumbling with the stubborn seat belts, and turn to face the man by the open door. He is standing on a box so that all of us can see his hand and arm signals. The noise level has effectively rendered all of us deaf.

After the last command, I can sense a lessening of the line in front of me, and am propelled forward by the crowd to my rear. I am forced forward at the same time that I realize I couldn't stop if I wanted to.

As I take my turn in the door, I can't help but think that *everything* here was bought from the contractor with the lowest bid. I feel the jumpmaster's forceful slap on my right buttock, and I step out.

WHY?

Why would anyone jump out of a perfectly good aircraft while still in flight?

# Chapter Two

This was supposed to be a high-tech brush war, if you'll pardon the apparent contradiction. We, the United States, were to use our military technology and weapons superiority to aid one of our developing third-world allies put down a growing civil insurrection, and in the process we would both help contain and stop the spread of communism in South East Asia. Didn't our high-school history and civics classes tell us that we had won in WWII and in Korea? In our biased over-confidence we had been led to believe that this little podunk country that no one had ever heard of should be no problem – after all, the majority of the insurgents had either out-dated or homemade weapons and no real leadership. The USSR and Red China didn't really get along well together, either, and were watching the U.S. involvement from a distance, we were told.

My method of transport to Viet Nam was evidence of the changing times. Our fathers were delivered to their war zones across the oceans, Atlantic and Pacific, in military vessels designed for troop transport. But my generation, (at least the group of roughly one hundred replacements of which I was one) got to fly over the Pacific Ocean, and in a chartered civilian commercial airliner, at that. We were flown from Oakland, California in a Boeing 707 belonging to Flying Tiger Airlines. With stewardesses and in-flight meals, to boot. We stopped in

Hawaii for a grand total of 15 minutes, and stopped at Clark Air Force Base in the Philippines for about one complete hour. Nevertheless, in just seventeen and a half hours of flight time we were landing in the Republic of Viet Nam.

My first impression of Viet Nam occurred, naturally enough, at night, which seemed to add to the mystery of the exotic Far East. We had landed at Ton Son Nhut Air Force Base, and as we disembarked from the plane down the rolled-up staircase the first things that we noticed, especially being in a climate-controlled airplane interior for so long, were the strange smells and the heat. Even though it was nearing midnight we could feel the heat increase as we descended the stairs to the day-heat-enriched tarmac, and the humidity was almost physically tangible (and here I had been thinking the humidity back at Ft. Benning, Ga. was oppressive!) And the smell was disturbingly strange – similar to a grass compost heap, laced with a citrus taste and a tangy flavor, reminiscent of cloves in a baked ham.

So we were now *in* Viet Nam, but it was nighttime and we couldn't *see* Viet Nam, just feel it and smell it. And as we formed up for another roll call to confirm the passenger manifest the air of mystery increased as several blue Air Force 44-passenger buses appeared to take us to our destination. There was something different about them but in the cold artificial light it was hard to decipher at first. But as we boarded the buses it became obvious – all of the windows were protected (?) by a heavy metal grillwork, or netting, that made one immediately think of prison buses. The driver said it was for the protection of the vehicle's occupants (here read him, and us) as it was fairly impossible for a terrorist to hurl a grenade or a bomb into the bus through a window.

"Toto, I don't think we're in Kansas any longer," someone quipped as the driver finished his explanation.

How true.

Once all of the buses were loaded, we took off. And the fact that we were in an area of hostility was further driven home by the escort service provided to our bus convoy – Military Police jeeps, with M-60 machineguns on gun-mounts were both leading and following the buses. It was strange, but up to this moment the idea of us being in an actual war-zone hadn't quite registered with the majority of us. But as soon as we saw the three-man MP jeeps, with real ammo belts in the machineguns and not training blanks, the point was driven home, to even the densest of us.

None of us inside the buses had any idea as to our destination, or even as to where we were, for that matter. We were inside, clustered around the windows and gawking like a bunch of awe-struck tourists, trying to see what Viet Nam looked like, even though we couldn't see too well in the dark. It appeared that our route took us through a dilapidated shantytown, with a curfew in effect, for no one was on the streets but us. All of the shop signs were in a foreign language, naturally, but occasionally we'd see a familiar trademark logo, like the Coca-Cola emblem, or the Standard Oil sign.

It was definitely eerie – no skyline or city lights to speak of, no buildings higher than two stories lining the streets, no people out and about, a strange pervasive smell everywhere, and our MP jeeps continuously running ahead of the convoy to position themselves at all street intersections that we passed. (To this day I don't know if the MP's were doing it for show or for real, but their actions that night definitely made an impact on all of us bus passengers!)

Finally the buses stopped and we were told to dismount the vehicles. As we staggered out of the vehicles we could see that we were in a freshly plowed and road-graded vehicular area, with a bunch of OD green tents alongside. There was planking serving as walkways in between some of the tents, giving warning of mud due to the freshly graded terrain. This primitive tent-city would come to be known as Camp Alpha when it was permanently established with buildings and all, but right now it was more like an old picture from the Alaskan gold rush days.

This was the 90th Replacement Battalion at Long Binh, commonly referred to as 'the 90th Reppo Depot.' All of the Army's transient military personnel and unassigned replacements would be funneled through here, with an individual and his MOS. (Military Occupation

Specialty) being matched up and assigned to the unit, anywhere in Viet Nam, that could both utilize him and needed him. This was on the outskirts of Saigon but we didn't know that yet. All we were aware of was that we were in a large mud hole and had to perform a lot of Mickey-Mouse make-work details and muster for four or five formations daily, hoping that your name would be called, signifying that you had been assigned to a unit and were on your way out of this place.

I was here for six days before my name was called and I was alerted for unit orders, pending being notified of a unit assignment.

Now remember, I had just finished the Army's jump school a month and a half earlier so I was still what they called 'gung ho'; that is, thoroughly imbued with the proper training outlook and a positive, confident attitude. In other words we were the invincible and elite paratroopers, serving on the cause of right in a hostile area on the far side of the world, and I still had to prove myself. Accordingly, I expected to receive orders for either of the two airborne units serving in Viet Nam at that time; either the 101st Airborne Division (the 'Screaming Eagles' of WWII renown) or the 173rd Airborne Brigade, a smaller newer unit serving somewhere in the hills.

These were the only army airborne units in Viet Nam at the time, all of the others being 'straight-leg' units, a derisive term among paratroopers for non-jump-qualified soldiers (those who never bent their knees prior to performing a parachute-landing fall, but instead walked straight-legged as regular infantry on the ground). And I wanted to be assigned to the 101st because of their history and tradition, and besides, they had the coolest shoulder patch in the Army!

So, of course I received orders to a different unit altogether – the recently formed 1st Cavalry Division (Airmobile). Word was, this unit was originally a jump-outfit, but had been equipped with hundreds of helicopters to move equipment and men anywhere, and was being observed and tested in Viet Nam and its jungles. This unit was currently deployed up in the mountains somewhere in the middle of South Viet Nam.

There were no maps for us replacements to view while we awaited orders, but those of us who had seen maps of Viet Nam remembered a small banana shaped coastal country that curved down to the left with a swollen bottom, or south. Simplistically, the military had sectioned it into four quarters, or Corps areas. Starting at the north, at the DMZ between North and South Viet Nam (the parallels to the Koreas was blatantly obvious, even to the densest of us) was I Corps, pronounced 'eye-core.' The I Corps was primarily U.S. Marine territory. Moving south, II Corps encompassed the mountainous highlands in the central part of the country, III Corps covered Saigon and the Mekong River from its entrance in Cambodia, and the IV Corps area was primarily the Mekong Delta, or the swollen 'bottom' of the banana. Rumor control had it that IV Corps was essentially underwater, either devoted to rice production, or comprised of vast marshlands as a result of the frequent floods of the river as it neared the ocean.

All of the barracks lawyers there at the Reppo Deppo kept talking about how the 1st Cav got its ass kicked in a huge ambush at the Ia Drang Valley and needed a large amount of replacements to fill its ranks, hence my orders. (In all actuality, the Cav had been there about a year and needed replacements on a regular rotational basis, and the Battle of Ia Drang had actually happened about ten months ago.)

Knowing from nothing as I did, I listened to all of these rumors with foreboding, and really did not think much of my future. I was also told that there was still one brigade within the division that was still on jump status, explaining why I was being sent there.

But helicopters? I'd been raised in the Pacific Northwest, where the Boeing Airplane Co. was a big employer in my hometown, and we were used to seeing all sorts of jets and airplanes in the skies, both as test flights and commercial aircraft either enroute to or departing from nearby Seattle-Tacoma International Airport. It was a rare occasion whenever a helicopter was spotted, and I could only recall seeing one but three times in my entire life – and they looked rickety and flimsy, and not very stable or airworthy at all. And I had received orders to a unit that was going to pioneer the helicopter and new tactics in a combat environment!

Truly, my big Adventure was in progress.

The next afternoon, after a morning of necessary paperwork details had been completed, I was bussed with several other soldiers back to the airfield. Here we waited for a C-130 to fly us to the 1st Cav Headquarters in the central highlands with the strange sounding name of An Khe. It seemed like everyplace in Viet Nam had a name of two words. It would take some getting used to.

The Airforce C-130 brought back memories of jump school, for this was one of the aircraft used for our qualifying jumps. This sense of familiarity was vaguely comforting, especially as I was heading to who knows what.

As it was, we did not fly straight to An Khe, but instead landed at another location in the highlands, with the strange name of Pleiku. We were told that we would be here overnight and would catch another flight in the morning, straight to An Khe.

Pleiku reminded me of the Northwest, my home. There were hills and mountain ranges, but no snow on them, and everything was green, really green, a lush, dark green that bespoke of healthy vegetation and trees. Other than that, I felt as if I were in or on a movie set, similar to one about the French Foreign Legion, for everything was strange, different and exotic. We were given a boxed C-ration for dinner, told to stay in a dugout bunker near the side of the concrete airstrip at Pleiku, and wait for morning. But sleep was impossible, due both to our excitement and the fact that some type of dark and foreboding combat jets would land and take off every couple of hours, on some type of mission. As they took off with the aid of their afterburners, the noise was horrendous. How does one get used to this, we wondered?

We were definitely in a war zone, the strangely darkened and camouflaged combat jets that prevented our sleep were proof of that, and they also made us wonder why a jet that flew high in the sky needed a jungle-camouflage paint-job, as it was parked on gray-white concrete when it was on the ground and looked like a jet, regardless of the paint! In our naïve arrogance, none of us thought about other enemy jets being *above* ours in the skies. And we still had no idea where we were. If we had been given a map none of us could show our location. This feeling of ignorance and dependence on others was remarkably unnerving.

When morning finally arrived, we were told to form up and wait for our inbound aircraft, the one that would fly us to this mysterious place called An Khe. This was also my first sight of the ungainly and spindly-looking CV-2 Caribou aircraft. This thing looked as if it was constructed out of leftover parts, had bent wings, and a fuselage that bent up to a high tail. I would later learn that this all-purpose aircraft could land and take off on a very short runway, and carry a proportionately heavy cargo. This airplane was in use everywhere in Viet Nam, but our first sight of it was less than confidence-building. As we watched it circle the airstrip prior to its landing several of us pointed it out to the others, for none of us had seen one before. In the air it resembled a huge, but slower, dragonfly. An immobile dragon-fly, frozen in rigor-mortis, for the wings did not flap, yet to us rookies it did appear to float in the air, slowly and gracefully, as it landed.

My first memories of An Khe are of a hot, bright sun, another military bus picking us up at a dirty airfield, and lots of gritty dust blowing in the breeze, or just appearing to hang in the air. The landing strip was not concrete, as was Pleiku's, but instead was composed of PSP. This was *P*ierced *S*teel *P*lanking, corrugated and ridged sheets of metal, pierced full of holes to make them lighter, about eight foot by three foot each, which could be laid down and interlocked like a child's Lincoln Log set. This was easier to lay down and set up, and repair, than laying or repairing a formal concrete strip. And faster, too! As a result of these characteristics, an airfield could be operational and able to receive landing aircraft within just a few hours of the start of the field clearing procedures. Also, it could be relatively quickly repaired after a mortar or rocket attack, by replacing the damaged sheets.

And due to my nervous expectations all colors seemed amplified – the sky was a startling blue with the whitest of white clouds, the various greens of the vegetation were absolutely vibrant and the brownish-gray dusty dirt of the makeshift roads seemed to sparkle in the sunlight.

Almost as an afterthought, scrunched into this bright vista of color, were what at first appeared to be hundreds of canvas tents which were eye-catching due to their numbers and their distinct lack of color – for they had originally been a dark forest green but with age, the effects of sun-bleaching and weather exposure, and the accumulation of countless layers of the all-pervasive brownish dust these tents were now remarkable for their drabness. And this was the military complex at An Khe, called Camp Radcliffe – at first glance a huge tent city, no permanent buildings to speak of (indeed, it seemed that the only wooden structures were the familiar and ever-present two and three-hole latrines that denoted specific unit areas), a hodge-podge of tent clusters that tried to adhere to some semblance of order in the crazy-quilt patchwork of roadways and company streets that really seemed to have no rationale in their initial layout.

This tent city, An Khe, was erected in the shadow of a huge hill or mountain that rose several hundreds of feet above the communal area. This was Hon Cong Mountain, and it became the familiar landmark of An Khe, for some engineering unit had constructed a huge First Cavalry shoulder patch just below its summit, on its military crest. This Cav patch was visible from any spot in An Khe, and as the military installation that was the First Cavalry's home base grew in size and complexity, the outer perimeter (called the 'green line' at all military installations and fire bases) kept expanding outward until eventually Hon Cong Mountain and its tourist-attraction yellow military patch were swallowed up into the grounds of Camp Radcliffe proper. The result was sprawled out before us now – a huge tent compound, with what appeared to be a semblance of order/disorder, erected at and around the base of a large dominating hill, with a gigantic yellow Cav patch at its top. All in all, a very impressive and visually stunning panorama for us to take in as our first impressions of An Khe.

Now, to all of this, we have to also add the one ingredient that made the First Cavalry unique in Viet Nam up to this point: its helicopters! In my first fifteen minutes' worth of bus ride from the dirt strip airfield I saw more helicopters than I had in my lifetime up to this point. It was almost like a science-fiction movie, for there was a busily intense, almost electric military activity everywhere in sight, standard trucks and vehicles evident on the roadways, tents galore spread out around a massive hill and all kinds of exotic looking helicopters flitting around like angry insects in the sky, with the resultant sounds hard to describe as the helicopters could and would fly with no apparent destination or purpose that was obvious to us spectators. If we watched an airplane fly, we could see in which direction it was going and kind of calibrate in our heads its flight path and the route it would have to take. But not with a helicopter! These things could go up/down, left/right, or nowhere and just hover in place, seemingly on a whim; some would fly in formations with others, and some would fly by themselves. And in the first five minutes of our initial helicopter exposure we must have seen five or six different types of helicopters, of all sizes, and some of them had cargoes suspended in netting or webbing dangling beneath them! Strange. And off in the distance we could see 'normal' fixed wing aircraft flying to various destinations at differing altitudes or in the traffic pattern at the airstrip where we had just landed. I remember one of the other replacements remarking that the only thing needed to complete the picture was the Goodyear blimp!

And as I recall, the one sound that I associate with An Khe is the sound of motor engines, be they gasoline or diesel. Vehicles on the ground, whether wheeled or tracked, and aircraft, whether they were fixed-wing or rotary-wing, and the hundreds of power generators to provide electric power to various unit areas, all of these had motors which were running continuously. The resultant din was a steady droning that one could gradually adjust to, just as a city-dweller learns to accommodate to traffic noise. But at first, the noise was overwhelming.

Those first few days at An Khe, and in the First Cavalry Division (Airmobile) are still a blur in my memory. But I do remember, foggily:

- being assigned to an engineering unit, the 8th Engineer Battalion. At first I was sort of non-plussed for I was green enough not to see how this unit would help me get into the Special Forces. The lights began to glow in my head when I was told that I was being sent to the Battalion Commo (Communications)

Section in the Headquarters and Headquarters Company (the HHC).

- not being able to recognize any of the radios that this unit was using, and also being told that I would now be an OJT (*o*n the *j*ob *t*raining) radio-teletype operator. Here I had been trained for an MOS of O5B, a Morse code radio operator, and the MOS for radio-teletype operators was O5C, which normally required an additional 12 weeks of training. But now I'm being told that this was the position I would fill, and I would learn as I go.
- going through the division's short, three to five day orientation for serving in a tropical area. During this refresher training of basic soldiering skills, and how this climate would affect them (and us), we were also issued the new jungle assault rifle, the M-16. This was a lightweight plastic and metal rifle, nicknamed the 'Matty-Mattel' space gun, that fired a 5.56 mm cartridge (akin to a .22 cal long) instead of the 7.65 mm cartridge (a .30-.30 for all practical purposes) that we were trained on in basic training using the M-14, the longer and heavier wooden and metal rifle in use throughout the military branches. First the radios, now the weapons are different – a trend is developing here!
- when issued clothing, the trend continued. We had to store our precious jump boots and were issued instead two pairs of the newly developed jungle boot, designed of rubber and canvas, with some leather to polish, that was intended to get wet and dry out repeatedly. Later, we would realize these boots were a godsend in the boonies, and during the rainy season.
- by the same token, we were issued jungle fatigues, designed to be large and loose to combat the heat, and of a material that was lightweight, durable and able to withstand repeated soakings, either of sweat or rain.

All in all, I began to realize that everything I had been taught, everything that I had been trained in or on, was not current or up-to-date here, in this unreal war zone which was to be my home for the next 12 months. I had better stay alert, I thought, and more importantly, I had better listen to the people who had been here awhile, for they would know things, wouldn't they? The oft-repeated phrase, 'by the book', did not seem to apply here, for there always seemed to be a different way to do things here 'in country', which was a catchphrase for being in Viet Nam. What I really needed to learn was who knew what they were talking about and who was just trying to sound knowledgeable, at their listeners' expense. In other words, who was bullshitting, and who was not. This would be a good trait to learn for any walk of life, not just here in Viet Nam.

*21 Aug '66*

*Dear Folks,*

*I finally got assigned to a unit. Remember when I said that I wanted either the $101^{st}$ or the $173^{rd}$, and not the $1^{st}$ Cav? Look where I ended up – the $1^{st}$ Cav, and in an engineering battalion, yet. But that's okay, since I'm in the Commo section.*

*When I reported here today, the communications sergeant showed me around a little bit. Funny, but they don't have a single radio here that I've been trained to operate. The Sgt. said everybody new here is the same way – they train on one bunch of radios, but we use a different set of radios out in the field.*

*They also told me something, which ticked me off – that I wouldn't receive any jump pay while I'm over here. So I went to the orderly room and asked the company clerk about it. He said that a lot of guys were not getting jump pay because they haven't put in for it. Then he started typing and asking me questions. When* *he finished I asked what he just did, and he said he typed out my application for jump pay. He also said that my chances were pretty good on getting it. I've got my fingers crossed, since it means an additional $600 that I know I can save while over here.*

*In case you're wondering, we're at a place called An Khe, in the mountainous region. It's pretty up here – all green. It reminds me of the area by Duvall and Monroe. Green hills (not too high) that are fairly green with meadows or lowlands in among them.*

*Mom was right – I brought the wrong Rosary, even though I like it. Send the black one as soon as you can, if possible.*

*It's getting dark, so I have to stop. I'll write again soon.*

*Love,*
*Jim*

So I learned to operate a completely different piece of equipment than the radios that I had been taught. In fact, as the name implies, a radio-teletype is more than just a radio – it was actually a typewriter that sent its signal over the airwaves. (For its time this was hi-tech!) The one that we used was designated the MRC-95, which was a radio that had both FM and AM capability, a modified typewriter keyboard, and a cryptography accessory box that encoded, or scrambled, the signal being sent out so that it was undecipherable unless the receiving unit also had a crypto box that was attuned to the transmitting unit's specific code. These crypto codes were declared to be unbreakable at the time and were changed every 24 hours. One needed a SECRET clearance to change the codes, or even open the crypto box, so for the first three weeks, I was not allowed to do this until my INTERIM SECRET clearance was approved while the appropriate background checks were being conducted.

Now the First Cavalry Division was an airmobile outfit, meaning that everything and everyone in the division was capable of being transported by aircraft. This meant that all vehicles in the unit could and would be airlifted either inside fixed wing aircraft or suspended in cargo netting under helicopters as a slingload. So all wheeled vehicles (jeeps, trucks, ambulances) were of a size that could be fitted inside airplanes or even the larger cargo helicopters, such as the dual rotor CH-47. This also applied to crew-served weapons, such as howitzers and cannons, the artillery pieces. If they could not be rolled inside an aircraft's hold, they were equipped permanently with lifting shackles, or attachment points, for the hooking up of nylon slings that the helicopters would then latch onto and sling-load the item underneath the helicopter as it lifted and carried it to its destination.

The MRC-95 radio-teletype was no exception. It could be installed inside a room or building as an inside fixture requiring only a steady and secure source of power, usually provided by an external five kilo watt generator or, as in our case, it could be mounted in a jeep (somewhat permanently) leaving only enough room for a driver, for the complete radio component took up the entire rear of the jeep and necessitated the reversing of the front passenger seat, to face the rear of the vehicle and operate the teletype keyboard. Once lifted and/or driven to its location, the jeep was then parked alongside and under a canvas tent (as in our case) and either the vehicle was then run to provide power for transmission, or a portable five kilo watt generator was installed nearby and hooked up to provide the necessary electricity.

I knew how to type. I knew Morse code. And I knew basic radio set-up, installation, and operating procedures. Period.

Now I started to learn how to be a radio operator for real. I was kept at the division's base camp in the engineer battalion's headquarters' Commo section and was taught to operate in both the battalion net, sending and receiving radio traffic from the companies within the battalion, and on the division net itself, sending and receiving radio traffic from the various unit headquarters within the division.

As a newbie, a cherry, a rookie in-country, this was an interesting phase for me. And exciting, to boot, for while I was learning all of the practical aspects of being a functional radio operator, while I was on radio shift duty I was almost required to eavesdrop on traffic from and between various units other than engineering ones, to include infantry, artillery, aviation and even the medical and military police on occasion. This exposed me to a different overall perspective than just that of an individual GI trying to get through his day – I also got to get a glimpse of the bigger picture as I got the feel of what different units were doing and what was happening in the various forward areas in the Cav's overall area of operational responsibility, or AO, as it was called.

*7 Sept '66*

*Hi,*

*Time for me to write again, so that you can't say I don't write often enough.*

*I'm not sure if I like being a radio operator, or rather, the hours that I keep. I'm on duty 12 hrs. a day for 7 days of the week. I'm on for 6 hrs., off for 12, then back on for another 6. It's getting to be a drag, to put it mildly.*

*Hey! We got attacked last Sat. night. The VC lobbed in about 50 mortar rounds at the airstrip/heli-pad (1/4 mile from where I was on radio watch). Result – 4 dead, 64 wounded, and about 47 aircraft damaged or destroyed.*

*For the first half hour of the attack, I was never so busy before in my life. I had 3 radios on different frequencies, and they were all busy at the same time – this guy wanted artillery support, this one wanted a Med-Evac, another guy wanted to report sniper fire, etc. In a way it was just like a war movie.*

*After we got our troops in their defensive positions, the other radio operator (2 on duty during attack) and I had to wait – either for the attack to let up, or for the shelling to reach the radio shack.*

*So while we waited, we played a game of 'Scrabble.' We couldn't leave our radios or go anywhere, and it did help to pass the time away. Now that I think about it, it does sound funny, my first time under fire I played a game of 'Scrabble.'*

*Jon [brother] would love it over here. It is absolutely the buggiest place I have ever been. There are all kinds and shapes over here.*

*In the same vein the weather here is different, too. So far it hasn't gotten unbearably hot, yet, but the humidity here is something else. It's a muggy, sticky kind of heat. Ychh!*

*Other than that mentioned above, this place isn't all that bad. But just the same, I wouldn't want to live here. I miss swimming too much.*

*Better go now. Will write again.*

*Love,*
*Jim*

Personally, I felt that I was stuck in the rear while Viet Nam was happening all around me. It was fascinating to read the daily sit-reps (situation reports) that were sent, in the evening, from all of the forward elements to the HQs in the rear. Reading various reports from the infantry units gave one impression, the aviation units another, and the artillery units still another one yet. Putting them all together in my head, rather like clues, gave me an idea of what was actually going on in the highlands area, at least as far as the Cav was concerned. And being young and gung-ho, and not really knowing any better, I began to feel left out, as if all of the military effort and activity, that one couldn't help but notice on arrival in Viet Nam, was occurring all around me, in spite of me, and that I was missing out on something important.

And from a strictly utilitarian sense, I now began to notice a growing respect and admiration for the Cav's helicopters and the Airmobile status developing within me, even though I had yet to ride in one myself. For transportation alone they were eminently suited for our highland region, with its distinct lack of airfields and insecure roadways. The airlift capability, both internal and slingload, was both practical and impressive. And as a weapon of war, of which I had only vicarious knowledge, their armaments and maneuverability were proving invaluable. The only drawback to this developing reliance to a new innovation was the simple fact that they were weather dependent – that is, they could not fly in the foggy, socked-in, low visibility conditions that generally accompanied the monsoons in the mountains, but then, neither could most fixed-wing aircraft. And they generally could fly to places that other airplanes and wheeled vehicles could not get to, even on a good day.

Also, during this time, I avidly read every copy of the *Pacific Stars and Stripes*, the official military newspaper, that came my way and received the propagandized version of the military's activity in Viet Nam. We *were* the good guys, we *were* helping the citizens of Viet Nam, and we were involved in something difficult and hazardous, but ultimately *morally* necessary. We could hold our heads up, and be proud later on in life, just as our fathers and uncles were of their war. This we gleaned from the reports and articles in the papers and magazines, we read it in black and white, so it *had* to be true, and we believed it. And disregard the protest movement that was developing back home. That was just a temporary and political aberration that would soon pass. After all, they weren't over here to see what was going on.

# Chapter Three

For the next five or six weeks I was kept at An Khe as the FNG (fucking new guy) in the Battalion Communications section. I tried my damnedest to learn this new radio, its characteristics and its method of operations. I knew how to type. I knew Morse code. And I knew what the Army taught in the basic radio operator's course. Period. And that was all I knew.

So I applied myself and attempted to listen to everyone who had some experience, both in the Army, and with a communications background. The Commo section itself encompassed both radio and telephones, called landlines, or 'Lima-Lima' in the vernacular of the military. So there were radio operators and telephone linemen, who also functioned as field-telephone switchboard operators, in this group. It was surprising, the extent of the knowledge that I began to acquire. This Commo section covered just about everything except electronic component repair. For this we had to send or deliver the defective or broken equipment to a higher echelon (here read more involved and technical) maintenance and repair battalion devoted solely to this task, always located at the rear.

I became familiar with the MRC-95 radio-teletype, its strange three row keyboard, with an upper and lower case for every key, unlike a 'normal' civilian typewriter. And I began to learn, and become effective, in radio procedure. I learned, through experience: how the weather and terrain could and would affect both the transmission and reception of a signal; field expedient methods of setting up various antennas to counteract this effect, hopefully; how an AM signal was more reliable than an FM one; and all of the various and sundry bits of knowledge that one should know, besides just talking into a handset as one would picture a radio-operator doing.

Throughout all of this I kept reminding myself that these people knew, and were taught, lots of stuff that I did not know. That I was being shown what I needed to know to become effective, on this particular piece of equipment, and in this particular piece of geography, Viet Nam. This concept of only knowing 'what works here' was peculiar to my whole Viet Nam experience – I always felt that I knew only enough to get by, that others in my field always had a more extensive background knowledge simply because they were 'school-trained,' a phrase that came to differentiate those who were more competent from those who were just OJT. (It took me years to realize that the majority of the competent and efficient Army personnel whom I encountered were *all* OJT themselves, in one aspect or another, at one time or another!) But at the time I couldn't shake the feeling of being second best, comparing myself to others who knew more than I did, and always trying to measure up.

As an example, on the division's net, at the end of the day various units would send their traffic in an orderly sequence, controlled by the receiving station, the division HQs, who acted as the NCS (the Net Controlling Station). My unit was always last in order, and I was always amazed at how fast the other stations could type and send their daily situation reports, or sit-reps. When I found out that my unit was last because we had to actually *type* our reports, and that the other units had teletype-tape machines like a stockbroker's ticker-tape machine, I really felt like a second-class cousin by comparison. These other operators would type their messages ahead of time, onto a perforated tape, and then when they were due to transmit just turn on their tape machine, which would then run the pre-typed tape, which in turn would send the message at a blurring rate of speed, compared to our manually typed transmissions. So no matter how fast I typed, or how proficient and accurate I became, I still did not even know what a tape-machine looked like, let alone how to operate one!

And I was still at the rear base camp, learning a job, so to speak, while I was in a foreign country, and in a war zone at that. We were restricted to our unit area, and only occasionally would I see a Vietnamese, and this was usually at the mess hall, which employed some local civilians, normally older women, in the rather mundane aspects of mess hall duty.

I truly felt that the war was going on without me. Especially so when I would listen in on the other units' reports, particularly the infantry, at the end of a day. The forward elements of the Cav were operating to the north of a coastal, port city called Qui Nhon (which was about 50 miles due east of An Khe) and just to the south of a place called the Bong Son plains. This was an area noted for its rice production, in essence one of the 'breadbaskets' of Vietnamese agriculture, akin to the U.S. Midwest farming region and the Russian Ukraine. This region was between the mountainous highland region and the coast of the South China Sea. It also straddled the main north-south highway that followed the coastline, called highway QL-1. The enemy at this time seemed to be doing their darndest to interfere with the production and transport of this staple crop, and was intimidating the civilians of the region.

So the Cav, along with the Vietnamese army and some units of Koreans, notably the "White Horse Division" and the "Tiger Division" were slugging it out with the Viet Cong in an attempt to clear out the enemy, or 'pacify' the region. And I was safe in the rear base camp, a non-combatant, but I was young and naïve enough to want to see what the war looked like. I had already been exposed to a couple of night-time mortar attacks, but An Khe was considered a 'safe' place to spend the war by several of the older NCOs. Indeed, the main target of the mortars appeared to be the aviation area where the bulk of the helicopters were parked, known as 'the Golf Course' for some strange reason that never was satisfactorily explained to me, other than that the berms that protected the helicopter parking stalls were like holes. But even I knew that there were more than 18 helicopters in that area. Besides, this helicopter-heavy area was way off on the other side of the huge base camp, so as of yet I had not begun to feel fearful, or have any sense of personal danger. I was just curious. And excited to be here after all.

Finally I was determined to be competent enough to be sent to the division's forward base camp. In the middle of October I was sent to LZ Hammond, still undergoing construction and improvements, located near the village of Phu Cat. This was about 30 miles south of the town of Bong Son.

*2 Nov '66*

*Hi,*

*Just thought I'd let you know I'm still around and kicking. I've been busy lately, and haven't had a chance to write any letters. Sorry.*

*Right now, I'm at a forward CP near some little podunk village called Phu Cat.*

*I say again that Viet Nam is pretty, and if it wasn't for this "war" out here, it could be called beautiful.*

*Rumor has it we'll be going to the Delta in February.*

*Gotta go. Promise to write again tomorrow or the next day.*

*Love,*
*Jim*

LZ Hammond had all the attributes of being an An Khe North. It even had a functional airstrip, constructed of PSP (pierced steel planking) rather than concrete. Air Force C-130s and the ungainly CV-2 Caribou were the primary fixed-wing planes that the airstrip could accommodate. There was even a huge hill in the middle of the camp that was reminiscent of Hon Cong Mtn. but as of yet there was no gigantic 1st Cav patch on it. Off to the west one could see the foothills of the highlands, to the east was a ridge of foothills, abutting the coastline almost, and we were in a large populated valley, but there were no civilians in this particular spot.

All of the vegetation had been effectively cleared or scraped away, creating a huge bald circle around the central hill, and this was LZ Hammond, both currently in use and also under construction. This was the Cav's forward base camp, sited here to service and re-supply all of the field elements that were conducting Operation Irving, if I recall correctly. There were numerous smaller LZs and firebases scattered all around, but this was the main military location for miles around.

And this was the beginning of my first monsoon season. I was raised in the Pacific Northwest, which had a reputation for an unusual amount of rainfall during the year, which had a direct bearing on the remarkable greenness of the region, which always impressed visitors to the area. So I thought I was used to rain. And I was, but not to a monsoon's drenching! This was a downpour that one had to experience to appreciate. It rained a lot, a hell of a lot, and it rained continuously, almost 23 hours a day, total. In one day we received over nine inches of rainfall.

And LZ Hammond, still under construction and improvement, plus the normal essential military activity one would expect at an installation of this size, had had all of its vegetation cleared. The resultant muddy quagmire is still difficult to describe. Suffice it to say that one could expect to stay wet and muddy for the next two months, if one had to venture outside at all.

But I didn't mind any of this at the time. For I was now no longer 'in the rear' but out in the field. I was excited. I felt as if I was getting closer to the war; my big adventure was on a roll! In fact, one drizzly morning the infantry units nearby were kicking off another field operation, and were airlifted from LZ Hammond to the hills to the west, performing one of the airmobile combat assaults that up until now I had only heard or read about. We stood outside of our Commo tent (a GP-Large, that we shared with the medics, housing the Bn. First Aid Station in the other half) drawn by the sound of helicopters, lots of helicopters. A helicopter, especially one in the rain, has a unique sound in itself, more than a few at the same time create an unmistakable din. We watched in fascination as 23 lift-ships filled with troops, and escorted by 10-12 gunships flying above and to the sides of this flying convoy passed overhead. Standing on the ground, watching, not really knowing what I was seeing – I have to say that it was thrilling and inspiring. We felt like we were a part of something, if only behind the lines, so to speak. Besides, as of yet that was more helicopters that I had seen in my life up to that point, let alone all in the air at one time – and in one single humongous formation, yet!

It was also at this time that the little cog (me) in the great war machine began to get oiled and polished and started to function, as it should. Teenager that I was, due to my upbringing I firmly believed that the way to grow into manhood was to do well while in uniform. So I continued to strive to excel and learn everything that I could. If I could type and most of the other units had teletape gizmos, then by golly I was going to be one of the 'fastest and bestest' manual Teletype operators. I was going to keep up!

I also developed a strong friendship with one of the telephone linemen, a native of Texas (with the strong southern drawl to prove it), and we built our own 2-man sandbagged hootch, or living quarters. This was a strange aspect of this conflict, for the Army provided enough tenting for all of the major functioning offices, but the troops were expected to build their own living areas. Similar to the concept of trenchline bunkers of World War I, except that we built up, and walled everything in with sandbags. After all, this was really a 'safe' forward base, and there were infantry troops to secure the perimeter. The only thing that we had to worry about was an occasional mortar attack, and there wasn't really anything in the engineer area to warrant targeting by the underequipped enemy. Especially when one realized that there were fuel and ammunition dumps, and aircraft, on the same installation, just not near us.

Our first little 'house' was not so good. We scrounged up some canvas and made a fairly comfortable two-man tent and surrounded it with a double wall of sandbags. It was good physical exercise but that was about all for when the monsoon rains hit, they seemed to hit with a personal vengeance, and our little hootch effectively flooded and dissolved in the torrential downpours.

Then we wised up. At night, when we were both off duty, we snuck over to the materiel storage area, and 'requisitioned' some plywood sheets and some engineer stakes, plus some plastic sheeting. This was all marked *Property of U.S. Army – For official use only.* We were *in* the Army. Hell! We *were* the U.S. Army! We did not consider it stealing at all. In any case, we jury-rigged a fairly waterproof box to live in, and sandbagged the heck out of it to hide the evidence. Except for the mud, which was everywhere, it was livable, private, and still a lot better than whatever the infantry troops out on operations had.

I continued to improve my proficiency on the Teletype, and continued to learn whatever else I could relating to radio. I also learned the rudiments of field telephones, simply by living with a lineman. Many nights, even in the rain, when I was not on duty my friend would ask me to go with him as he searched for a break in the line. So I would hold a flashlight and rifle while we backtracked the line (Commo wire) from the switchboard in the Commo tent to the unit who had no telephone. Somewhere between us and them the line was severed, usually by a vehicle running over it or some such. As we never left the base, it was never dangerous, just muddy!

In a few weeks time I had progressed to the point that my Commo Sgt. both recommended me for a promotion to E-4, and appointed me as a team chief, actually in charge (or so I thought) of the teletype rig and its three-man crew. It was good for my ego, but I still felt as if the others knew a lot that I didn't. The proudest I ever felt was when during one radio shift the NCS reported, after I had sent him our daily sit-rep, that his unit didn't receive my entire transmission, and he requested that I *send my tape again!* I could hear his mouth drop open over the airwaves when I replied that I had no tape-machine, but was typing it by hand.

*3 Dec '66*

*Hi,*

*Here I am again. I forgot to tell you that the weeks are longer over here than they are back home. Anyhow, I'm writing the letter that I promised you.*

*There's not much of anything that's happening over here that warrants any mention. Except –*

*If it rains over here just one more day I swear I'll start quacking like a damn duck. Just 4 days ago we got 9" of rain in a 24-hour period. And to think that I didn't join the Navy because of my fear of drowning!*

*The rain has washed out all the roads into our location for 10 - 15 miles in all directions, but they were dirt roads anyhow. So for the past 5 days they've been flying in gas, ammo, and all supplies by plane. There's about 10 planes landing a day now.*

*Hope you get the Christmas card okay. They flew them out from base camp (An Khe) and passed out as many as they could. It's sort of a hokey, patriotic Christmas card, but it's the only one they had.*

*They just confirmed the report that if you extend for 6 months over here you get a free 30-day leave, plus travel pay to any location in the free world. I wouldn't mind extending for 6 mos. as a door-gunner, and going to Denmark, France, or Switzerland for*

*30 days. By that time I'd have $1000 saved and I could have one heck of a good time.*

*Of course, that's the way I feel now. By the time my 12 mos. are up, I'll probably be in such a hurry to get home that I won't even give it a second thought!*

*And I think that I told you that I'm a team chief now. And I didn't even go through Teletype school. What's even funnier is the fact that I'm just a PFC, and a team chief is supposed to be a buck sergeant. I just may get an early promotion. Ha! No such luck.*

*By the way, if, when I get home, anybody, but anybody, mentions that we should go camping, eat outside, and just enjoy the unbounded wonders of nature, I think I'll punch him in the nose. Brother, you can have it! (Make sure that you warn Uncle Leonard, even if he does out-rank me.)*

*Tell Barbara [sister] to write a letter, and that I'm still waiting.*

*Right now we (I) closed down the net (went off the air) and I hunted on the radio's 28,000 channels and lo! I found a station from Melbourne, Australia. So now we're listening to the Top 20 in Australia and Britain. It's the first music I've heard since I left home, and it sure has changed. I'm going to memorize this frequency, 04.982, for future use.*

*I've just about run out of things to say, so I better start wrapping things up.*

*I miss you all, and wish I was home, sure, but it's pretty interesting over here so I haven't started to get homesick yet. But give me time.*

*Merry Christmas.*

*Love,*
*Jim*

*P.S. Get our men out of Viet Nam - send women!*

And because we worked in the same tent, I also became friends with several of the medics. They had their aid-station, and cots for their living area (no hootch for them!) with wooden pallet flooring in one half of the GP-large, separated by a heavy drop cloth to shield them from our lights, as our radio was manned and on the air 24 hours a day. My mother was a nurse, so I took an interest in their patients and symptoms whenever they had any business come through their door. It was usually construction-related injuries, with occasionally a few weird infections and fevers – but then, this was considered to be the tropics, and to be expected. Just the same, it was interesting and it also provided a break from the Commo routine.

I was beginning to feel the confidence of youth. I was learning communications knowledge as it pertained to Viet Nam. But I still listened to the older NCOs as they related their overseas military experiences, mainly in Europe. The two locations they kept referring to were the countries of Germany and Turkey. Germany was considered 'good duty', and Turkey was a good experience that made them appreciate other things, that were normally taken for granted. And whenever they started to bring up things 'by the book' or 'according to the manual' I felt that they had some secret knowledge to impart. For I was still new enough in the service to really consider myself to still be a trainee, less than 10 months total service, and about two of those were actually leave – and besides, I had never even seen this manual that they kept referring to. And they had read it! And would quote it! So this was continuing to add to my personal quandary – even though my competence was improving, and my confidence was building, my lack of formal training and the experience factor of others more knowledgeable than I was also contributing to my feeling, and fear, of inadequacy, of not being able to measure up.

On a more positive note, the young tourist within me felt as if he were released from confinement and was finally given the chance to view the 'real' Viet Nam, not just the military build-up. As our activities at LZ Hammond became more regular and routine, the area commanders authorized visits, or passes, to the town of Qui Nhon, about

20 miles to our south. This was received with great enthusiasm by all of the troops, regardless of their unit, as a chance to play was welcomed by all and really improved the overall morale. So the way the rotations worked out, we averaged one long afternoon every 3 weeks, unit duties permitting.

Some went to get drunk. There were bars and cafes everywhere, it seemed, and there was no such thing as being 'under-age' as long as one was in uniform. For many this was their first introduction to alcohol, and also the resultant hangovers. But at the time this was considered as one of the milestones on the path to manhood, and was a lynchpin of the military mystique.

Some went to get laid in any of the numerous brothels and cat-houses that spring up in all war zones. For many this was their first introduction to sex – I was one of these, and noticed a distinct lack of romance in the mechanical workings of sex. I'm sure my inherent nervousness and the language/cultural barrier contributed to my less-than-ideal first memories.

Others went just for a chance to break their routine and a chance to play tourist, and perhaps pick up some souvenirs. For this, it seemed that the whole of the Vietnamese countryside was prepared, not just the merchants in Qui Nhon. Roadside stalls were everywhere, selling all kinds of flimsy trinkets, photos, and beer and Coke. This was also our first contact with a war-time, black market economy as Cokes were being sold for fifty cents each, and cans of beer (American brands, by the way, originally destined for various military supply depots) for a dollar apiece. Their big selling point was that they were *cold*, a godsend in this weird country's even weirder climate of hot and wet. When one realizes that the average rice farmer would be fortunate to clear $35 a month, we were told, the impact of the war's inflation was patently horrendous on the typical civilian and his family.

As we hitched rides in any available vehicle headed that way, usually a three-quarter ton truck or a deuce and a half, the cameras came out and snapshots were taken of roadside dwellings and religious shrines, rural scenes centered around the ever-present rice paddy with its attendant water-buffalo, and the local inhabitants with their various modes of dress. The most talked about in the latter category, at least among the younger, newer in-country GIs was the rural cultural habit of chewing betel-nut, which dyed or stained an individual's teeth black by the time they appeared to be 30 years of age or so. This fascinated everyone who happened to notice that the person they were talking to had apparently healthy teeth, just unnaturally black. Until one became used to this, the black teeth did cause one to stare!

And one specific incident concerning Qui Nhon sticks in my mind. As we were walking down the streets of this tropical city, dodging mud and mud-puddles, I noticed a couple, apparently man and wife, with cameras out, clicking away just like typical tourists. But this couple was Caucasian, and stood out from the crowd for this simple reason. We later found out that they were French tourists, whose ship had briefly stopped at Qui Nhon to resupply and refuel. And this struck me as one of the oddest things about this whole conflict – why would any civilians want to visit a combat zone on their vacation? I was still too new in-country to associate the idea of historical French colonial rule and the resultant French influence on French Indo-China with the Viet Nam that I was currently observing. It took awhile to appreciate the significance of French influence, but later on as it sunk in it was evident everywhere – in the language, in the architecture, the Catholic religion, and the school system – all evinced French and European influence.

*5 Jan '67*

*It's about time for me to write again, so I will.*

*Both Christmas and New Year's have come and gone, so life is slowly returning to normal. All of the lights and decorations have been torn down; the stockings have been put away til next year, and all of the children are delighted with their extremely realistic rifles, hand grenades, muddy boots (similar to those worn by the T.V. soldiers) and other toys passed out by that insecure fat man with the crazy, red uniform. Funny. But since everybody started playing with their Christmas presents, they all look very much like soldiers. Sort of hard to believe, isn't it?*

*But in a more serious vein, I'll never forget this Christmas for as long as I live. And just because of one reason – the Christmas Mass that I attended.*

*About the only thing that this mass had in common with Mass at home is the fact that most of the "audience" were Catholic.*

*The altar was made out of ammo boxes. It was the first time I ever attended church wearing a canteen, first aid pack, 150 rounds of ammo, a steel helmet, and carrying a rifle. The service was held in a briefing room, constructed of sand bags. The crucifix, such as it was, was hung over a relief map of our immediate area. The altar had two 4 in. candles (I was surprised to learn that they <u>were</u> pure beeswax). The vestments worn by the priest were not the colors of the season, but were camouflaged O.D. The priest washed his fingers with water only, no wine. The altar boy (?) poured the water over the priest's fingers and into an <u>ashtray</u>. During the sermon, one of the candles went out. Christmas carols were coming out of a tape recorder set on top of a sandbag. The sermon was about how different a communistic way of life differs from ours (sort of a religious pep talk- "get out and win one for the old Gipper"- that sort of thing).*

*But just the same, it was the best service I have ever attended. And I know that I'll never forget it. Nor do I want to.*

*I have to go now, so tell Barb she owes me a letter.*

*Love, Jim*

Then the Christmas Holiday season arrived, and with it a re-affirmation to all us fledgling youths that being in uniform and serving our patriotic duty was the correct course to manhood. Due to our age grouping, and current events of the time, I've already alluded to the steady diet of film and television fare that we were raised upon. And this conflict seemed to fall in step with our pre-conceived ideas, and ideals, that we all held regarding warfare, if for no other reason than for the temporary cease-fires that were agreed to and implemented by the warring factions. This was the stuff that we had read about in school; this was the stuff that all of our male relatives talked about; and now we were a part of it.

I refer here to the honor among and between combatants. Recall the safe passage granted to all contestants, regardless of their home city, during the religious festivals culminating in the Olympic Games in ancient Greece. Recall the temporary truces between the Blue and the Grey at Christmas during the American Civil War, when both sides laid down their rifles, sang Christmas carols, and just enjoyed being alive. Recall the First World War as troops in the trenches, regardless of nationality, laid down their weapons on Christmas Eve to again sing carols and, on occasion, to actually exchange gifts: often tobacco, coffee and sugar, according to folklore.

And now we in Viet Nam were undertaking the same patterns. Never mind that my unit was composed of non-combatants and that the true measure and personal impact of a cease-fire was lost on us! The forces of which we were a part were acting according to traditions with which we could all identify, and which we believed were honorable. Never mind the fact that this happened to be an Asian country – there was still a large Christian populace (again, the French-Catholic influence) that understood the import of this particular religious season. So a temporary truce was declared, both for Christmas and New Year's Eve, during which no troop movements or aggressive acts were to take place.

So, imagine our shock and chagrin when we realized, in our naiveté, that of course 'the other side' did not adhere to the rules of the cease-fires, and instead took this as a perfect opportunity to move troops and supplies, without the fear of coming under fire. There were even numerous shooting violations reported in the *Stars and Stripes*, initiated by the other side, of course. These reports solidified our perceptions that the other side were 'the bad guys' and that they had no sense of honor. Of a necessity, this also reinforced our beliefs that we were the good guys, as were our fathers and uncles in their wars.

Regardless, come New Year's Eve, at midnight, I attended, just by virtue of being in Viet Nam, the largest and loudest light show and fireworks demonstration of my life. It seemed that every guard post, on every firebase, LZ, guard-mount on all bridges, and anyone with a weapon took this occasion to celebrate. The night sky, from horizon to horizon, was chock full of red tracers seeming to float lazily along their trajectory, parachute flares casting flickering sterile white lights over the countryside, causing shadows on the ground to seem to move as they descended, and multi-colored signal flares arcing up and burning out ferociously before they returned to the ground.

Visually, it had been magnificently impressive, yet one couldn't help but wonder what the average Vietnamese citizen, or rural inhabitant thought. After all, there had been armed conflict continuously in this country since before World War Two. And it was becoming increasingly obvious to us Americans that the enemy here knew how to wage a war on the cheap, without wasting his precious assets. But after our New Year's Eve 'shoot 'em up' one began to wonder if our side would learn this, as well. For we had an over-abundance of assets, and our mind-set was that this alone was enough to eventually win this war. Didn't the final outcome of WW II hinge on materiel and logistical superiority? But still…

Just as I was beginning to really feel competent, to be earning my keep, as it were, in mid-January 1967, we got alerted that the Cav was going to move its Division Forward base to Bong Son, in a move that would effectively consolidate its forces in Binh Dinh province. They were pretty scattered in a helter-skelter pattern up to now. The new headquarters were to be located at LZ English, an already established military installation which was sited several miles to the north of the Bong Son River and town of Bong Son.

Even though this was an Airmobile outfit, we ended up moving by vehicular convoy, for a distance of about 30-35 miles. We followed the main coastal highway, QL-1, and up to this point this was the most exciting military undertaking I had participated in. Not only did I drive the teletype-rig, but also the Commo Sergeant was my only passenger. The rest of the Commo group was split up among two other ¾-ton trucks and a deuce and a half, due to the amount of gear we had. We even had air support – a Huey gun-ship periodically flew over the convoy about 50 feet above us, and this was the closest that I had been to a helicopter thus far.

As it was, it took us the entire day to travel this fairly short distance. We had to stop once while some road mines were cleared ahead of us, and this gave us a chance to play while we waited. There were some coconut palms alongside the road and we knocked down a couple of coconuts. They were still green, but we cracked them open anyway, to taste the milk inside, just to say that we did. It was bitter to the taste, but an experience was gained, nevertheless.

As we neared our destination, we crossed the Bong Son River and got our first look at the town proper. The town was actually the market-place and mercantile center for the agricultural populace living in and farming on the fertile plains area sandwiched between the central highlands' foothills and the seacoast to the east. This was a junction of the Bong Son River flowing east to the sea, the highway paralleling the coast, running essentially north-south, and also the remnants of the national railroad, also running north-south.

The railroad bridge was about one mile south of the town, and off to the side of the vehicular highway. It had been blown up and effectively rendered useless years ago during the earlier conflicts, and the rail system was not operational now anyway, so there had been no effort to repair it. As it was, the bridge was a stunning visual reminder to the physical destruction generated by warfare, even though we ourselves had as yet to experience anything more than a random, impersonal mortar attack. But there it was – a destroyed concrete railroad bridge, just like in the war movies on which we were raised. At the very least it made for a good snapshot to send home to the folks, for inclusion in a photo scrapbook!

I liked the Bong Son area more than Phu Cat (LZ Hammond). A lot more!

The most obvious difference between the two bases was their size: LZ Hammond was a self-contained little military enclave, whereas LZ English was large enough that it actually straddled the civilian highway. (Just in total acreage English was about three times larger than Hammond.) In effect, there was LZ English and English East. The smaller English East was, as the name implies, on the eastern side of the road and was home to a couple of helicopter squadrons and the 1/9 Cavalry, really a unique infantry battalion which also had some helicopters assigned organically to it. The bulk of the forces assigned to the 1st Brigade and the 1st Cav Head Quarters, with all of its attendant support units, the 8th Engineers included, were on the sprawling complex of LZ English proper. There was even an operational airstrip in the middle of English, which could accommodate the majority of all fixed wing aircraft in use. And of course, the Division's helicopters were flitting constantly between the two halves of the total complex, or going up and down the length of the valley to any one of several firebase-LZs strategically located at various points within the expansive terrain that now comprised our new AO, from 'the mountains to the sea.'

The complex was about six miles north of the town of Bong Son, and there were many dwellings and local habitations alongside the roadway, with numerous 'neighborhoods' off on arterial roadways and side paths all throughout the main valley. There was even a little village right there at the main entrance, or gate, where local establishments like laundry services seemed to sprout overnight. The overall effect was that this installation was much more 'open to the public' than was the one we had just left.

And the valley was expansive enough that one never had the

'enclosed' feeling that was the norm at Phu Cat. The hills of the highlands rose majestically several miles to the west, with rolling lowlands for several miles seaward to the east. In fact, off to the west the one north-south ridge forming the beginning of the highlands proper was in all reality the eastern side of the notorious An Lo valley, a well-known VC stronghold and staging area for all of their raids in the Bong Son region. But from the vantage one had at LZ English, those mountains looked so peaceful and serene in the distance!

But primarily, I must admit now, the weather had a hell of a lot to do with our first impressions – for the monsoon season was over and the sun seemed to be out continuously now. And it was hot. And it was dusty. Specifically, there was no trace of mud anywhere – no puddles, bogs, or quagmires that anyone who had spent any prolonged amount of time there would of course come to associate with LZ Hammond. The entire valley was under cultivation of some kind, well-tended rice paddies and their enclosing, criss-crossing dikes covered the valley, and even the roadways were elevated on sun-baked and age-hardened earthworks, or berms. The resultant effect was one of dry preparedness. A most welcome change, to be sure!

Most importantly, and not to be overlooked for its simple obviousness, was the ample evidence of vegetation throughout the entire complex. Palm trees, bushes, vines, numerous trees of unknown identities, underbrush, and all sorts of exotic grasses were everywhere throughout and all over both halves of the LZ. It looked like the only intentional clearing of brush had occurred at the green line perimeter, for fields of fire just outside the concertina rolls that formed the barbed wire barriers. Indeed, it seemed that the burgeoning military site was growing among the vegetation, and not competing with it. It simply felt more *comfortable* here at LZ English than it did at LZ Hammond.

*27 Jan '67*

*Hi,*

*We moved to Bong Son. That's why I haven't written lately. We got sort of confused preparing to move. When we finally did get under way, it only took 6 ½ hours of steady driving to go 33 miles. The roads (?) are bad.*

*It was a pretty safe convoy. We had air support most of the way. Just the same we had a little dab of sniper fire and found some mines in the road. I like the area around Bong Son a heck of a lot better than Phu Cat. It's not as secure here, but the scenery is really beautiful.*

*Remember that French correspondent Michelle Ray? They found her car and body about 2 miles up the road a couple of days ago. She got her story about 'the other side' all right. Trouble is, she never got a chance to write it.*

*The Bong Son River is a couple of miles south of here, and the South China Sea is about 6 miles to our east. I am going swimming, as soon as it's safe.*

*We have no idea as to how long we'll be out here. We were supposed to be at Phu Cat for just a 'short while' – we ended up staying there for 4 ½ months.*

*I got a letter from Gene [a high school friend, serving in the Navy Seabees] the other day. He's already gone on an R&R to Hong Kong. And he also goes home about 3 months before I do.*

*Remember California Joe? The one in San Francisco who I went to jump school with? I finally got in touch with him, and he says that he was at Phu Cat for awhile, but I never knew it. We rotate home at the same time and he wants me to stay at his place for a couple of days. I think I will. Bag the European ski trip – it was a nice dream while it lasted.*

*Gotta go – am running out of paper. Write soon.*

*Jim*

In any case, it was here in the Bong Son region that I really felt as if I was coming into my own, so to speak, as far as being a knowledgeable and competent member of the armed forces. I felt confident about my ability to function as part of the Bn. Commo Section, both as an RTO and as a Teletype team leader. I was proficient in my duties, I knew enough to be comfortably in charge and responsible; and I had the energetic optimism that I was learning more about 'my radio' every day. In short, I was gaining the personal satisfaction that one gets from doing or performing a task well.

There was even a chance to play, here. The Brigade's wash point, for personal laundry and pressurized hoses for the cleansing of vehicles was down at the Bong Son River. Equipment had been installed to siphon water from the river, and to purify it for drinking or filter it for cleaning. There was even hot water for a shower facility. Best of all, I thought, there was an area of the river that had been designated as okay for swimming. It was amazing what a fun dip in the river could do for one's attitude and overall morale. So a laundry run to the wash point became a treat, rather than just another dutiful chore. And our vehicles began to stay a lot cleaner, too!

Even though our round-the-clock Commo duties made us feel as if we were confined to our duty areas, these laundry runs also gave us a chance to get off base and to see the countryside. Within the five mile distance to the wash point, we saw a representative sampling of Vietnamese country living, urban life, and the effects of the recent conflicts upon the populace.

Both the recently completed and the currently ongoing military operations being conducted on the Bong Son plains and the adjacent highlands resulted in a large portion of the area becoming what the military and the government euphemistically called 'pacified.' This actually meant that whole villages and hamlets were physically relocated from their homes and farms to a safe area. This was usually akin to a large relocation camp that resembled more a barracks area and a prison than the rural habitations from which these people had been removed. They were often located just off the main highway, and as we drove by it was obvious that the 'internees' here, for lack of a better word, were not really as happy to be there as the officials cared to have us believe. Idle peasants with sullen stares, looking through the barbed wire fences 'erected for their own protection' could not be misconstrued as anything but what they were – unhappy to be there, and wanting to go home! The entire An Lo Valley had been de-populated in this fashion and had been reclassified as a free-fire zone, due to the VC strongholds still operational up there. It was patently obvious to us, especially as non-combatants, that this misguided de-population policy was being misused and was probably swaying a lot of public opinion to support, or at least be sympathetic to, the other side. Throughout my entire stay in Viet Nam, I could never shake the impression that the average peasant couldn't care less about which government or party was in power in Saigon – all he wanted was to be left alone, to tend to his crops in order to take care of his family.

It was at about this time that I realized I was passing an unexpected checkpoint on one's path to maturity, or manhood, or just plain personal growth. Here I refer to the bittersweet aspect of personal sadness of having to say goodbye to a close friend, and yet having it offset by a sense of gladness for the well-being of that same departing friend. My friend from Texas, the telephone lineman, had completed his year in Viet Nam and rotated home. I was very glad for him. But I felt very alone after he left. I missed him terribly, and was not even aware of it until a couple of other friends mentioned that I was acting out of sorts.

As we talked about it I began to realize that there was a downside to building friendships. This was to be a recurring problem as 'the musical chairs' concept of personnel turnover and replacement came to affect everyone in Viet Nam, regardless of their individual unit or branch of service. Invariably one would develop a strong personal friendship with one or maybe two other individuals, much more intense and intimate than we had been used to in our schooldays with the requisite 'group friendships' associated with either a school-class clique or sports teams. It then became a rugged and traumatic event when one would leave. Traumatic for all concerned – for the one leaving would feel both elation at the idea of going home and guilt at having to leave his close friend(s) behind; whereas the one(s) remaining would feel conflicting emotions also as they felt glad for the departing friend, yet also feel an almost selfish sense of loss and unfairness as they remained in-country.

I honestly don't know if there is a 'correct' or 'socially appropriate' behavior pattern or procedure to follow in situations of this sort. I do know that if there is I never discovered it, or was never informed of it. But I do know that I saw this scene repeatedly and went through it myself several times during my stay in Viet Nam. It got to the point where one could notice it in phases – a) the build-up, where the parties involved would become unknowingly short-tempered and irritable with each other as an impending DEROS date drew near, b) the physically-separating event, as good-byes were said, usually involving an evening party the night before an individual actually departed a unit, and, c) the mourning phase, as the people remaining behind in-country tried to be brave over the absence of their close friend, and others could only observe and give them space and time as they dealt with it and eventually came out of their funk.

One could, over time, become inured to this process – but one *never* got used to it! And it never became easier. Not for me, at least. The coping mechanism that I resorted to was to become increasingly self-reliant, 'surface-friendly' with many, yet increasingly intimate with only a select few. It seemed to work. It got me through. But as the years passed I noticed that this particular behavior pattern unwittingly led to a sense of isolation, of feeling 'alone in a crowd' as it were, as the select few seemed to dwindle in number and disperse over distance and time.

*1404*
*DE RA E-4*
*-M- 040200H APR 67*
*TO THE FAMILY*
*FM JIM*
*BT*
*U N C L A S S I F I E D*

*HI,*

*THIS TIME I HAVE AN EXCUSE FOR NOT WRITING – I JUST GOT OUT OF THE HOSPITAL. NOTHING REALLY BAD, JUST TENOSYNOVITIS. YOU KNOW, A SCREWED UP FINGER. MIDDLE FINGER, RIGHT HAND. IT WAS SWOLLEN BAD SO I WENT ON SICK CALL AND THE DOC ABOUT HAD A FIT BECAUSE I WAITED SO LONG. HE SAID THAT THEY WOULD SEND ME BACK TO AN KHE AND CUT THE WHOLE FINGER OPEN SO IT WOULD DRAIN. BUT WHEN I GOT TO THE FIELD HOSPITAL ONE OF THE DOCS WANTED TO PUT ME ON ANTIBIOTICS AND SEE IF THAT WOULD HELP ANY. I HAD A BAD FINGER ON THE END OF MY ARM, SO THEY FILLED MY REAR END WITH PENICILLIN AND STREPTOMYCIN AND KEPT IT FILLED. I'M BACK IN MY UNIT NOW BUT MY FINGER IS STILL TOO STIFF TO PULL RADIO SHIFT. SO I'M PULLING MIDNIGHT TO 6 FOR A SOLID WEEK SINCE THERE USUALLY IS NO TRAFFIC PASSED DURING THIS PERIOD. RIGHT NOW THE FINGER IS TOO BIG TO WRITE WITH, SO I'M USING THE TELETYPE TO WRITE THIS LETTER, TYPING WITH MY LEFT HAND.*

*REMIND ME TO NEVER GO TO A FIELD HOSPITAL IN A COMBAT ZONE AGAIN. SAW THINGS I DIDN'T*

*WANT TO, AND HEARD THINGS I SHOULDN'T HAVE. WILL TRY LIKE HELL TO FORGET. SORT OF MAKES A GUY WAKE UP AND BECOME AWARE OF LIFE – THAT THERE IS A VAST DIFFERENCE BETWEEN LIVING LIFE AND JUST EXISTING.*

*HEY, I'M GOOD! BE PROUD OF ME! A COUPLE OF DAYS BEFORE I WENT TO THE HOSPITAL I PULLED A JOHN WAYNE. FOR A COUPLE OF WEEKS OUR UNIT HAS BEEN BUILDING A "ROAD TO THE SEA" FOR SOME TANKS TO USE AFTER THEY WERE LANDED ON THE BEACH. BUT NOBODY KNEW WHEN THE TANKS WERE COMING. THEY WANTED A RADIOMAN ON THE BEACH WITH A RADIO TO CO-ORDINATE THE LANDING OF THE TANKS WITH THE SECURITY FORCES ON THE BEACH TO PROTECT THEM FROM AMBUSH. OUT OF EVERYBODY IN THE BATTALION, GUESS WHO THEY SENT? REAL HUSH-HUSH. THEY LET ME KNOW THAT I WAS NEEDED A WHOLE HOUR BEFORE I WENT OUT. I HAD TO ASSEMBLE ALL THE PARTS TOGETHER FOR AN ANTENNA TO MAKE SURE IT WAS COMPLETE, GET A RADIO BACK-PACK, AND GET INTO MY GEAR - ALL IN 1 HOUR. THEY FLEW ME OUT THERE WITH SOME VIETNAMESE SKIN DIVERS WHO WERE TO SEARCH THE WATER AND BE SURE IT WAS CLEAR OF MINES. FLEW OUT THERE IN A CHOPPER AND RODE BACK IN ONE OF THE TANKS. GLAD THAT I'M NOT A TANKER. NO SPRINGS.*

*WOULD YOU BELIEVE THAT IT IS HOT OUT HERE? IT GOT UP TO 101 DEGREES YESTERDAY. THAT'S HOT.*

*BY THE TIME YOU GET THIS I SHOULD BE IN BANGKOK, THAILAND. MY R&R GOT APPROVED. I*

*JUST FOUND OUT TODAY. I'M GOING TO TRY TO GET A STAR SAPPHIRE RING. THEY ORIGINATE IN THAILAND.*

*I SHOULD BE HOME SOMETIME IN JULY. I'M EXTENDING AND I GET MY CHOICE OF WHEN I WANT THE 30 DAYS. JULY'S A GOOD MONTH – EVERYBODY HOME FOR VACATION. MIDDLE OF SUMMER, AND WATER-SKIING. IF I DIDN'T EXTEND I WOULD COME HOME AUGUST 12 BUT THAT IS A LITTLE LATE IN THE SUMMER TO REALLY PLAN ANYTHING.*
*GOTTA GO. LEFT HAND'S TIRED. WRITE SOON.*

*LOVE,*
*JIM*

*BT*
*KKKKK*

*NNNNNNN*

This was also the time within my tour that I became eligible for an R & R. This was a five day out-of-country vacation that actually amounted to a week and a half away from one's unit when the travel time and processing time were factored into the equation. All personnel, regardless of branch of service, considered this to be the high point of their tour. Married personnel would meet their spouses in Hawaii, or perhaps Japan, while all of the singles would opt for one of the exotic cities of the Orient that were part of the program, and promptly spend their five days as an affluent tourist in the city's notorious flesh-pots.

This policy worked out well for all concerned – the participating cities would gain an influx of readily spent cash, and the military personnel would experience an incredibly prurient five days that one could not begin to conceive of back on Main Street, Hometown, USA! I had listened to others as they extolled the merits of different R & R locations and as a result I put in for Bangkok, Thailand. So of course they sent me to Manila, in the Philippines. I did not mind a bit! Anyplace would have been good, as it was a chance to totally block out the experience of Viet Nam, if only briefly. I also told myself that this was a chance to see a part of the world that, in all probability, I would never see again.

My memories of Manila are varied – I hardly remember any of the food that I had to have eaten; I remember playing with the flush toilet in the hotel room, as I re-acquainted myself with both the contraption and the idea of all that wasted water; I remember being terrified by a taxi-cab ride, where everyone driving on the roadways seemed to have a death-wish, and traffic rules were non-existent; I remember going to a movie theater and having to stand at attention prior to the film's showing as both the Philippine and American national anthems were played; and of course I remember my feminine companion, who acted as both courtesan and tourist guide for my entire stay.

When I returned, back to my unit and my duties in Viet Nam, I was almost a 90-day loss. This term signified that an individual was within three months of rotating home. I had done a lot of thinking, had done a lot of listening to others as they talked about the preponderance of 'Mickey-Mouse rules' that one had to contend with, on a stateside duty post, and figured that after the devil-may-care, lax disciplinary attitude that one both encountered, and adopted, in Viet Nam, that it would probably be a good idea for me to stay there a while longer! So I decided to extend my tour in Viet Nam for another six months. It was a good bargain, really. I got a free, non-chargeable 30 day leave for extending, so I figured I would actually be there an extra five months. I had a safe job, liked my duty assignment, and got along well with everyone, so I would not have to learn a bunch of strangers, for another six months at least. Plus, I was saving money (a rarity in the service!), and I would also get the bonus of another R & R with my additional six months in-country!

In the second week of May 1967, not more than four or five days after my request for a tour extension had been submitted for approval through the proper administrative channels, I was called into the battalion's HHC orderly room. I figured that there was some paperwork snafu or other, concerning my extension. My section's Commo sergeant, whom I liked and got along well with, was there when I arrived. But he had a strange look on his face, and I knew something was up.

He was holding a handful of papers, and told me that I had come down on an internal division levy, and was being re-assigned. And that there was nothing he could do to stop it. I had been assigned, in my original MOS of O5B, to a new unit that he had never heard of before – the division was forming a Long Range Reconnaissance unit, and that was to be my new home, while I remained in Viet Nam.

Although I was a non-combatant, a chaotic bombshell had just been dropped on my regulated little world.

# Chapter Four

Long Range Reconnaissance! I had no idea what that was, at the time. And neither did anyone else that I went to, seeking any information that I could get. Nobody could offer any help. But simply the name alone was exotic enough to sound romantically exciting, and really fired up my imagination. And anyone else that I mentioned it to.

The trouble was, that was all anyone knew. Nobody who worked in the orderly room had ever heard of it, other than the orders received for me, indicating that it was a new provisional unit in formation and it was located back at An Khe. The unit designation was mysterious enough, by itself, to cause speculation – HHC, G-2, LRRP Detachment, 1st Cavalry Division (Airmobile). That was a mouthful, but here is how it was broken down:

HHC - the *main* Headquarters and Headquarters Company for the entire division. It was explained to me as similar in function and location as the Oval Office for the U.S. Presidency.

G-2 - this was the Division's Intelligence Section, impressive enough in itself! As an aside, G-1 would be the Personnel and Administration Section, G-3 would be the Operations Section, and G-4 would be the Logistics and Supply Section. And, if extant, a G-5 would be the Psy-Ops (Psychological Operations). Again, these were the sections (or staffs) that functioned directly under the Division Commander, much the same as a Presidential Cabinet, and serving the same purpose – the smooth and orderly running of the division. In a similar vein, for smaller units like battalions and brigades, these staffs or sections were designated S-1, S-2, S-3 and S-4 to differentiate them from the larger ones.

LRRP Detachment – intriguing in that it was not a normally designated unit name, such as platoon, company, battalion or regiment. This meant that it was an abnormal unit, of indeterminate size, detached (attached, actually) to either the HHC of the Division or the G-2 Section. We couldn't tell which from the unit's address, as written, and that seemed to make it all the more curious and tantalizing to the clerks, who were supposed to be able to decipher all of the military lingo and gobbledy-gook that passed their desks.

And then there was the name of the unit – Long Range Reconnaissance Patrol. I was inundated with everyone's guess as to what this meant. Remember that I was currently in the division's Engineer Battalion, so all of their suggestions were based on their idea of unusual or irregular combat units. Their guesses alone were enough to scare me, but the name of the unit simply appeared to be self-explanatory, so I took it to mean just what it said. I just did not have any infantry background or combat experience with which to reference it.

Regardless, the only option open to me was to prepare for a move in compliance with these new orders. The military regimen made it an easy decision for me, for I could not disobey. I had no idea what I was getting into, but I had been conditioned to prepare myself wholeheartedly for surprises such as this. Besides, it was exciting enough just to wonder why I alone had received the orders and no one else in the unit. But then, at the age of 19 years I suppose everyone feels that they are unique and special. And all of the training I had received so far reinforced this belief – at radio school we were smarter than others, at jump school we were more courageous and better disciplined than others were, and here in the First Cav our division was outperforming many others. Just like being on a team in high school athletics, *we* were better than *them.* (This insidious competitiveness was not apparent, nor even noticed until later in life, as one looked back on events that one experienced, and their impact.)

In any case, there was going to be a drastic change in my immediate future. But then I had joined the military not really knowing what to expect, other than it would be different and more challenging than anything I had been used to. My Adventure (with a capital 'A') was definitely continuing, and gaining momentum.

So there was nothing for it but for me to report back to An Khe. It's all fuzzy in my memories as to the exact chain of events that ensued. I don't remember going back, whether it was by air or by vehicle, and I certainly don't remember signing out of the 8th Engineer Battalion, even though I had to have done so. And I can't recall just how I got to the LRRP area, but here my memory does kick in.

The LRRP Detachment was sequestered off by itself, seemingly in quarantine, at a place called "LRRP Hill." It wasn't until much later that I was informed that the unit was isolated for training and security purposes; for reasons of instilling and maintaining unit integrity; and that the unit's location and even its existence was not to be carelessly broadcast about.

This was off on the far eastern side of Camp Radcliffe, and the 'company area' was on the far side of the hill, effectively shielded from both the view of the curious and from the normal hustle and bustle that was occurring in the steadily improving divisional base camp. Believe it or not, there was even an amphitheater-like stage erected in an open field that was used for touring USO shows. This stage area was on the camp's near side of a large hill: this was "LRRP Hill" to those of us in the know. Out of sight on the far side of this same hill, approachable only by navigating a very steep, dirt 'jeep path' (the word *road* seems inappropriate here) was the quarters area of this mysterious and reclusive LRRP unit. My first thought was that they apparently liked their privacy.

I do remember my first few minutes, my very first impressions, as this was definitely the strangest image I was ever to receive of any military organization, in my life.

As one came up the hill on the only road, the road gradually curved to the left, like a switchback, and continued on just below the military crest of the hill and ridge on the far side. Following the road as it turned hard left, one first saw a GP-Medium tent to the right (this was the Medic's tent, both a workplace and his living quarters). Continuing up the road just 75 meters, on the right was a large cleared and graded area where several GP- Large tents were eventually to be erected. There were five in use when I reported in – one for the Montagnards assigned to the unit, two for the LRRPs already there, and two for the training class, of which I was to be a part.

To the immediate left, from this spot in the road, was what looked at first glance to be a large unpaved vehicular parking strip. In actuality this was the unit's formation area and where my training class would eventually do their crack-of-dawn morning calisthenics.

Still standing in the same reference spot, as you looked past and directly uphill from the formation area, you noticed a couple more GP-Mediums, several conex containers, and a couple of generators to supply electrical power. This was the unit's orderly room, Commo center, and officer's area. Standing there, holding my duffel bag and gear, looking uphill to the orderly room, is my first recollection of the LRRP unit, and I couldn't help but notice that this road in the making continued on the ridgeline into the trees, and seemed all the more mysterious as there was nothing there, on the back of the hill. A road to who knows where? And I was…?

I went to the one tent that opened onto the road. It had to be an orderly room, as it had a wooden porch facing the unit compound. Besides, I could see a desk in it from where I was. As I approached the tent, I couldn't help but notice an older man with a beer-belly, wearing cut-off military pants and sandals, along with a bamboo hat, lying in a lawn chair and drinking beer. He flipped his hand casually as I inquired if this was where I reported in to the LRRP detachment.

Now remember, I had just left a unit where discipline had been enforced, and I wasn't to realize just how Mickey-Mouse it was until much later, with more experience behind me. As an example, it was a punishable offense not to be in uniform, such as having your shirt-sleeves still rolled up after 6:00 PM. "Countermeasures against malarial mosquitoes" was the official explanation. And here was an older individual, definitely out of uniform, and drinking beer right next to an orderly room! What kind of a unit is this? And what about authority? I remember wondering to myself.

As I was doing some kind of paperwork in the orderly room, with an equally improperly dressed company clerk, he informed me that he was a Sgt. E-5, because I could not guess his rank. I hesitatingly asked who the guy was, outside the tent, who had waved me in.

"Him? That's the First Sergeant. I see that you've already met him."

With that response I just knew that I was in a far different unit and place than I had been accustomed to so far. But then, in May of 1967 I had only been in the Army almost 18 months, and the Engineers was the first and only unit that I had been assigned to. Damn, but I still had a lot to learn!

The other first impression that I have of this strange LRRP outfit still brings a grin to my features, but nevertheless it really emphasizes that I did not know what I was getting into, and shot my personal anxiety quotient up off the scale.

While I was still signing in at the orderly room, I realized that this outfit was what the name implied; that it was formed specifically to field teams to gather information and hard intelligence, much in the same manner as the old frontier scouts of American Western lore.

And as I was in the tent, an individual walked by the tent's front, said "Good morning, Top" to the First Sergeant in the lawn chair and kept on going around the tent. Now this guy was big! I was only 5'6" when I stretched, and for four years in high school I was the shortest one on the football team. Maybe not the lightest, but definitely the shortest. So I was used to playing with the big boys. But this guy was huge! He was shirtless, was wearing some kind of strange camouflaged cloth pants that I had never seen before, and his skin had been darkened by the tropical sun – but he still looked like a hulking gorilla posing as an NFL linebacker, or vice versa, to me!

I looked to the clerk and asked him who, or what, that was that just went by.

"Oh, that was SSG Torres. He's our Commo sergeant."

*Commo sergeant! My God! If that's their Commo sergeant, just what in the hell do their field troops look like?* I thought to myself.

What am I doing here? And just what am I getting into?

Over the next three days the rest of the training class trickled in, from all over the place, it seemed. They came from various units that were scattered all over the First Cav's TAOR. And as they continued to arrive I began to feel more and more out of place. I was one of only three radio operators in a class of approximately 42, and all of the others were infantry. And to make matters worse, from my perspective at least, they were all experienced infantry, as evidenced by the tales they related to one another as we got to know one another in the tents.

Here I had thought that I had been anxious before, when I first reported in to the engineering unit and had to learn a new radio set-up and its procedures. Now I was going through what amounted to a career change, as I realized the exact nature of this new LRRP unit and what my responsibilities would be. I would still be responsible for the radio, as a LRRP team's RTO. But in addition to my basic duties I was expected to be cross-trained in all of the other team-members' duties and responsibilities, also. In the back of my mind I kept thinking of the Special Forces brochures that I had picked up at the Post Office, a lifetime ago. This outfit, the LRRP Detachment, was operating on the same principle – independent and self-supporting six-man teams, with every man able to fill in for another. It was kind of gratifying to realize that I was getting what I had originally wanted in the service, but it sure was a circuitous route I had been given, and I was still coming in through the back door!

The more that I listened to these guys and their war stories, the more determined I became to learn all that they knew. They may have had infantry-training back stateside, but they, like me, had come to realize that everything that they had been taught did not necessarily work, or work well, over here in Viet Nam. They admitted that on several occasions their old tactics and methods had to be scrapped, and that they had to follow the advice of several personnel who had been in country long enough to learn new things. In any case, I reassured myself that if I could learn a new radio rig and its procedures well enough to ultimately become a team-chief, without the benefit of school training, then I could certainly pay attention and learn all that I could here, about the infantry and the LRRPs.

So here again my personal anxiety quotient was rather high as I admitted that I would be in an OJT situation again! But this time it was different, for not only would I receive the formal training that I would need to perform and function well as a LRRP, but I told myself that I had a bunch of experienced classmates that I could learn from as well. Another motivating factor, though it sounded absurd, was that this time it was for real – I was not 'playing war' with the kids in the neighborhood anymore, but would be doing it for real, against people who had been doing it for years, and who would not hesitate for a moment to kill me if they got the chance.

But I also observed something rather peculiar about this group of trainees that I belonged to. First, I had to admit that I was excited about being here and that I liked the idea of me becoming a LRRP, regardless of the effort and challenges that lay ahead. I was enthused, if not gung-ho. But the majority of the others simply saw the training ahead of us as further time 'out of the bush' for them. They were still in Viet Nam, but during the training phase they would not be 'humping the boonies' and getting shot at, as they put it. In effect, they considered this to be part of their 'get-over time' where they could actually relax and play. As experienced infantry vets, they had a perspective that I could only wonder at.

When I mentioned this difference in personal outlook to several of them, almost to a man they all gave me a sardonic grin and said that I'd learn, in time. Sadly, I have to admit that they were right; for I did learn. I eventually learned just how valuable and precious 'sham time' or 'get- over time' was considered to be, by combat vets, in Viet Nam.

Also, of the 42 or so of us in the training group, all but two were bona-fide 90-day losses. We were all short. It seems that the CO of the LRRP Detachment, a Capt. James, had finally been give the proper authorization to augment the unit's strength, which consisted of two operational teams at this time, by requesting, or drafting (stealing, actually) certain personnel and critical MOSs from the division at large. This did not sit well with the administrative personnel or the field units themselves, so they fought back in the only way that they could – they had to comply with the division-wide levy, as it had approval of the Commanding General, so they released to the new LRRP Detachment only those people that they were going to lose in 90 days anyway. Or their duds.

The upshot of this was a training group that was understandably glad to be back in the safe environs of An Khe and Camp Radcliffe, and was collectively cautious enough, due to their time already spent in the field, to have the proper attitude to be a LRRP. Trouble was, as soon as they would finish their training and complete two, or maybe three, missions they would be ready to rotate home. The 'musical chairs' aspect of a 12-month tour in Viet Nam was being felt again.

But once more I felt as if I was the exception to prove the rule – for I had already extended while I was still with the Engineers back at Bong Son. And I liked what I was seeing here, in the LRRPs, so I cautiously went to the orderly room. I had to admit to myself that I was still enough of a REMF that I associated the orderly room as officer country, to be avoided at all costs if possible. Capt. James and the First Sgt. (Kelley, I believe) were not there, but a Lt. Hall was. So I explained to him that I had extended in another unit but wanted to extend in this one, instead. He understood, and told me with a smile that once I was in the LRRPs I was not getting out, even though it was supposed to be an all-volunteer unit – that my original extension had been amended to reflect duty with the LRRPs. To this day I don't know if he was joking or not, since I was young and green enough to think of officers as another higher class of soldier, and duty in the Engrs had conditioned me to avoid contact and conversation with them whenever possible.

In any case, this was a further motivational factor or inducement for me to do well: I was going to be around for awhile, whereas the bulk of the training group would be going home for good shortly.

But just what kind of a unit was this new LRRP Detachment? And why would I want to extend my tour in Viet Nam for another six months in a newly forming unit, when I hadn't even completed my training for it? And what kind of training was going on? In essence, what was the draw, what was the appeal of this group that had me so thoroughly hooked, so early on?

In a word, common sense.

The more that I learned about the LRRP operational concept the more convinced I became that I had finally found a military combat unit that operated on the premises of logic and common sense; one that used the ideas that worked and discarded the ones that didn't, regardless of their currency in the military of the moment, or regardless of the fact that they were being utilized as authorized and conventional tactics world-wide for the U.S. Army. "Mickey-Mouse" was not welcome, nor allowed, in the LRRPs.

In effect, this unit was going to function in Viet Nam, and in Viet Nam only. Further, they were going to use the innovative ideas and alternative methods that had been proven effective in Viet Nam, whether the conventional forces adopted them or not. This particular conflict, this war in Viet Nam, was far different than any of the conflicts encountered in World War Two or the Korean War. This, in a nutshell, was what appealed to the independent renegade that was the true essence of being a good LRRP – we could be different, and get away with it!

The Long-Range Reconnaissance Patrol Detachment would operate, as I understood what was explained to me, in much the same manner as the Special Forces A-Team that had drawn me into the service in the first place. But the LRRP team would be a 6-man team instead of 12: there would be a Team Leader (TL), an Assistant Team Leader (ATL), a RadioTelephone Operator (RTO), a team Medic, and a Front Scout (FS) and a Rear Scout (RS). The Lt. in charge of training continually emphasized just how important were team unity and team integrity, that the members of a team be used to one another, be able to anticipate their responses. Even to the point that once a team was established they would not take substitutes or fill-ins, just to field a team for a mission. So if a man was sick or on R & R, for example, the remainder of the team would stand down until his return. This practical no-nonsense bit of common sense is, I think, what impressed me the most.

To further add to the romantic image that was already forming in my mind, the two scout positions would not be filled by American soldiers. Rather, they would use indigenous personnel, or Vietnamese natives, as scouts since they were already familiar with the territory. And here the LRRPs would go one step further and not use the Vietnamese soldier, which no one really held in high regard, but instead would use the Montagnard. The word *Montagnard* came from the French language and meant "mountain people." They were not Vietnamese, but were there first, apparently, much like our Native American Indians were there first, and there was no love lost between the Vietnamese citizens and the Montagnard population. Indeed, many years ago the Vietnamese Emperors used to go on "Montagnard hunts' for sport. The racial and ethnic distinctions, and antagonisms, still existed between the two population groups.

The LRRP unit had about 20 or so Montagnards, from the Rhade tribe, and they were an impressive bunch. They were always happy and smiling, were ferocious fighters, and had and did live in the mountains (the highlands) and were expert woodsmen, from whom we could all learn. They were officially in the South Vietnamese army, but had duty with American forces, and were all paid the equivalent of a Vietnamese sergeant, roughly $50 or so a month. The Montagnards assigned to us had their families at a village in An Khe, and it was a treat for the LRRPs to go there. I never got the chance, so I never met their families, just the scouts that we worked with.

So one can understand just how and why we all glamorized our role of intelligence gathering and began to think of ourselves in much the same vein as the Calvary scouts of old in the American Western

Frontier. All we needed to complete our mental picture were the buckskin jackets, with fringes, that the frontiersmen wore.

Here, again, this minor detail was taken care of, for in lieu of the buckskin outfit we would be wearing what was called "Tiger fatigues" at the time. The standard issue jungle fatigue was designed for tropical climates, true, and was durable in the bush. But it also looked like a uniform, which it was, and was easily identified as such. To make it easier for us to hide and blend into the underbrush we would be clad in a pants and shirt-jacket of a very durable cloth that was camouflaged black and green with dark brown traces that was not a standard issue item in the military's inventory. Indeed, we had to buy our own, at about $10 a set, off of the local economy. The best ones we purchased from the Montagnards, who got them from God know where. If we bought them from a Vietnamese merchant they were invariably a dark blue and green camouflage, instead of black. It became a matter of pride, eventually, to wear 'black Tigers' instead of the 'blue' ones.

So that completes the picture, of how we were composed as a team and what we looked like. But just what was it that we were supposed to do?

Our sole mission was to gather intelligence and information. The drawback here was that we were to do it *way out in the boonies,* where there were no friendly forces nearby to come to our assistance, should we need it. So we were taught the first rule of being a LRRP: avoid any enemy contact, in order to complete the mission. This was just fine by us! For a small force of six men was in no position to engage in a shooting contact with the enemy. Especially when we were normally outside the range of protective artillery fire, and it usually took our helicopters 30 minutes or more to reach our location. Just realizing that you are on your own for at least 30 minutes after the shooting starts is enough to make even the densest of us not want to pull a trigger. Ever!

So we were taught to hide, to blend into the vegetation, to feel like we were part of the landscape. This may lead into some tense and hairy situations, with the enemy very close nearby, but that was our goal – to complete the mission. If we were sent out on a five day or seven day mission, or longer, then that's just how long we planned on staying. And we would radio back any pertinent information as we encountered it in the bush, and every member of the team, minus the Montagnards, would attend an exhaustive debriefing after the team was extracted, to minimize the chance that any detail might be overlooked.

This grown-up version of the child's game of hide-and-seek appealed to the majority of us, for some unexplained reason. Whether it was the challenge of not being caught, or the chance to legitimately exercise some youthful bravado, I'm not sure. But there were various scare stories being circulated among us trainees, by our trainers, about some of the close calls already experienced by the two standing LRRP teams!

But the underlying message was still very evident – stay in the bush, stay hidden, and complete the mission. Shoot only if you absolutely have to.

We got the message. Loud and clear.

As stated earlier, the team's primary mission was the acquisition of first hand intelligence and information. This pertained both to the area and the terrain in which we were patrolling while on the mission, and any and all items of info which alluded to an enemy presence in, usage of, or passage through the area. In short, we recorded and ultimately reported everything that we observed and encountered. The Intel boys back at the rear would then correlate and/or decipher it, melding it into the larger overall picture within which the division operated.

From a physical and geographical perspective we were taught to record all unmarked trails on the map, and due to the foliage and tree cover there were plenty of these that were not visible from the air. We recorded the height and diameter of trees, location of streambeds (important when later occupying units needed water sources, or had to contend with these in the rainy season!), gradients of hills and ridges, sites of possible LZs, areas of bad or impaired radio communication, and anything else that might possibly be of use to any force that might have to operate in that particular area.

From a human perspective we were, obviously, to observe for any enemy in the vicinity, and note just what their activities were. As long as were undetected we could spy from a fairly safe vantage point and report back continuously as to just what the enemy was up to. We were usually patrolling at the far limits of the TAOR, or else we were in areas that were devoid of any allied presence. As a result, the enemy did not expect us to be there, and many times we would watch enemy groups congregate, record their numbers, observe their departure and call in their direction of travel, thereby giving warning to the rear HQs so that they would be prepared for unwelcome company.

By the same token, the *absence* of any enemy activity in an area also provided good Intel, for then we would know where the enemy was not! These were the missions that we all hoped for, for then they just became extended 'camping trips.' As long as we could joke and make light of our job, it didn't really seem so scary. But it did make for a rather grim and laconic sense of humor.

We knew what our job was. We knew what we'd look like in order to do it. And we had an idea, roughly, of who would do what, in order to accomplish the mission.

The three-week training regimen that we then had to undergo was designed to make sure, to make double-damn sure, that all of us would be able to effectively function in whatever individual roles we were assigned. More importantly, the training's overall focal point stressed the idea of teamwork, of individual cooperation to promote teamwork, and in effect took the idea of the military's 'buddy system' up a notch to emphasize that the team was paramount in importance. We all became fast friends and learned to count on one another, but this intangible, abstract entity called a team seemed to develop a life of its own, as it were, and each team that was fielded seemed to develop its own personality and characteristics, based primarily on the individuals that composed its make-up.

Ultimately, we came to identify more with the team that one belonged to, among ourselves within the unit; whereas to outsiders we appeared to be a detachment of LRRPs that comprised various teams.

This has been the ideal function of a LRRP team, so far. But what, as they say, if we got into some 'heavy shit'? What happens then?

For this contingency we felt that we were very well trained. We were taught compass and map reading techniques, exhaustively, so that every member of the team had a map and was to know the team's location at all times. Hand in hand with this skill we were also taught how to call in and adjust various artillery units, both on the gun-target line and the observer-target line, and to make on-the-spot adjustments accordingly. We even spent some time, a couple of days, at the artillery range, practicing. I'm sure, in retrospect that the artillery units that we used also benefited from this. Normally, an artillery Forward Observer (Arty FO) was an officer that accompanied an infantry unit, solely to provide artillery coverage for the unit. Of course, we all got swelled heads when we realized that any member of a LRRP team, in theory, should be able to also do that.

I mentioned various artillery units. There was the normal artillery (cannons, to a civilian) and in the First Cav there was also the newer Aerial Rocketry Artillery (ARA). These were Huey helicopters mounted with twin rocket-pods on each side of the aircraft, each pod capable of carrying 18 of these 2.5-inch rockets, giving each bird a maximum capacity of 72 rockets. These would be aimed and fired from the air, under the control and direction of the unit on the ground (us). These were highly accurate, and lethal, whenever we were within their flight range. Their passes, or 'gun-runs', were also faster and more accurate against an enemy on the ground than were the conventional artillery pieces, who had to reload and adjust from a good distance away, giving our mobile enemy targets ample time to move away from the impact area!

That was weaponry, from a distance. For our own personal armament each man had a rifle, and each team also had at least one M-79 grenade launcher. Most teams carried two, and really did not begrudge the extra weight or inconvenience, especially if they actually came into play!

And the rifles that we used were not just the Matty-Mattel M-16s either, for we also had access to a number of the smaller CAR-15s. These were essentially a shorter version of the M-16, with a collapsible stock, that was originally designed as a survival weapon for jet pilots who had to eject from their aircraft: it was short enough that it could be strapped to a pilot's thigh, prior to his ejection. Our usage of them was for the front scout and several of the forward team members to carry them, as they were excellently designed for 'boonie-bopping' without getting snagged in the vines and whatnot one encountered in the dense foliage.

(As an aside, several teams armed their Montagnard front scouts with captured AK-47 rifles, used by the enemy. The Montagnard, not being Caucasian and armed with an enemy weapon, would cause any enemy who happened to encounter him to take a second look. This momentary pause gave "the edge" to the LRRP team, and the front scout; for anyone that we encountered in our AO was definitely the enemy, but they were just not expecting us to be there in the first place!)

Now just in case anyone got hurt, either by the enemy or simply by Mother Nature (our camping trips, in a jungle, were really not simple walks in the park at all!), we were all given extensive first-aid training. This training even impressed the vets in our training class, who had had occasion to see field medics in action. We even gave IVs to one another, and took blood samples. This was done so that all of us would feel comfortable administering Serum Albumin, a blood expander to prevent hypo-volemic shock due to loss of blood. The more training that we obtained, it was noted that the more confident we felt out in the bush, knowing that our teammates could and would take care of us, if necessary.

Truly, the idea and concept of team integrity was catching on. Plus, the more we learned, the safer we felt; knowing that you were with better trained personnel does wonders for one's confidence level. Subconsciously, we also found ourselves trying harder – we wanted to measure up to the high standards we were being exposed to. I heard several fellow trainees talking in the tent one night, expressing a concern that they didn't want to go back to their old units for their remaining time in-country. They felt safer here, with the LRRPs!

Far-distance positioning of troops, and adequate re-supply of same was a luxury inherent to the airmobile concept. To us, one of the downsides to this was the fact that these helicopters could, and did, take us to the far boundaries for many of our missions. Way out there! But still, riding in a helicopter sure beats walking, most of the time.

For those areas that either the steepness of the terrain or the density of the tree growth did not afford an adequate LZ, we were taught to rappel from the choppers. This training was fun, and took place in the large open area where the stage and amphitheater were constructed, on the 'public' side of LRRP Hill. We were taught to rappel so that it became second nature to us. Indeed, a snap link and section of rope, to create a rappel seat, was a part of our uniform for every mission. We were also taught how to rig the helicopter, with a donut ring and four McGuire rigs, for the emergency extraction of a team through the forest canopy.

The rappel training was especially memorable, at least to my class, for the Scout Dog Platoon had asked to share our aircraft for their training. We had heard of these crazy guys, through the grapevine, but none of us had ever expected to see a handler and his dog rappel from a helicopter! The dogs were truly unusual in their trust of their handlers, and the different combinations of harness-hookups was fascinating. Remember, they were getting used to working with helicopters also, and they were still doing some experimentation, to see which set-up worked best.

It goes without saying that we had a rather physically demanding job, which required a lot of mental discipline. The mental discipline our trainers expected of us could be found internally. But they were there to help us with the physical aspects of being a LRRP. For this they would share their company with us for an hour every morning as they led us through daily physical exercises.

I thought I was in shape. So did the guys that had been humping in line units. But our training cadre did not think so, and went out of their way, I thought, to prove it. I did okay with the daily exercises and the running routine, but the hardest event for me was the graduation march. This was a forced march, in uniform, with an uneven, lumpy rucksack filled with 40 pounds of sandbags. We had to march the entire green-line perimeter of Camp Radcliffe, in a set time period. If one did not make it within the prescribed time limits, one would not be accepted into the LRRPs, regardless of how well one did in the training classes and exams up to this point. They even weighed the rucksacks at the end of the march, to determine if anyone had cheated. I ended up double-timing most of the march, just to keep up with my longer-legged classmates.

But I finished.

And I graduated.

Now I was a fully trained, qualified LRRP. I was now ready to be assigned to a team, for my first missions.

*2 June '67*

*Hi,*

*Remember when I first came into the Army how I wanted to be in the Special Forces or some comparable unit, where I could depend on myself and others who knew what they were doing?*

*I'm in it now. I'm now in the middle of my training for the 1st Cav LRRP. That stands for Long Range Reconnaissance Patrol. And in seven days I'll probably go down to Nha Trang for the Recondo School. That'll make me a Recon commando.*

*Now don't go off the deep end and get all shook up. I don't want you to. I'm finally in an outfit that I want, and I'm happy. You should know that. One reason that you shouldn't worry is that we are all highly trained and know what we're doing. It's not as if*

*I'm green and just got here. It'll be rough, sure, but I'll like it that way.*

*I suppose I should say more about our training and what we'll be doing.*

*They are teaching us to fire and become familiar with just about every weapon there is (U.S. and other), from a .38 pistol to a Sten gun with silencer. We'll even shoot crossbows.*

*They are giving us first aid and medical training that you wouldn't believe. Yesterday we gave shots to each other, and took blood samples from a teammate so we'd know how to give an I.V. injection. Today we learned how to cut the throat below the voice box so a man can breathe if his face is blown away. It is not, but is similar to, a traecheotomy (sp?). On patrol, we'll even have pep pills to keep awake.*

*We are being given extensive map reading and compass reading so there is no possible chance of our getting lost.*

*We're taught how to call in air strikes, artillery, and ARA (Aerial Rocketry Artillery) on a target by using encoded map coordinates.*

*We're being taught the Vietnamese language by an interpreter so we'll be able to talk fluently with anyone.*

*I'll carry an itty-bitty five pound. Radio, with a voice range of 60 miles, and a code range of 600 miles.*

*We're taught wood-lore to the point that we can be in an area for seven days undetected. We also know how to live off the land – eating snakes, beetles, roots, etc.*

*We can rappel down cliffs, make rope bridges, and all that good stuff that'll come in handy.*

*What do we do? Our job is just what the name means – Reconnaissance. We go into an outlying area where there are no U.S. or friendly troops, or haven't been there in a long time. And we scout.*

*We observe everything. The people of the region, vegetation, soil formation, any and all buildings, water potential, and all that. All our information is sent back, given a classification priority, and incorporated into all the maps & information given to U.S. troops who may go into that area.*

*And our main job is to look for Clyde. We report all enemy troop movements, locations, types of personnel and armament, - and we try to stay hidden.*

*More often than not we're dropped in by chopper. Sometimes we may parachute, or use rafts if we use water.*

*If nothing else, I'll be able to go hunting with Uncle Leonard without making a fool of myself and acting like a city-dude.*

*And they say that within the next couple of months I'll have my Vietnamese jump wings, along with my American jump wings. That I like.*

*Like I said, I'm going to like it. Right now we're doing the same job that the Special Forces did when they first got over here, before they switched to advisor status. I'll tell you more about it when I get home.*

*Believe it or not, I think that I'll like it so much – that I extended. Yep, no foolin'. Now don't go rantin' and ravin' and get all bent out of joint, because this is what I want. I know what it's like and what I'm getting into. I guess I'm just a glutton for punishment. Don't you go start worrying, since there's no sense both of us worrying.*

*I've got to stop now because I've said too much as it is. Besides, I'm tired, and need my sleep. I will be in top physical shape when this training is over.*

*See you in August.*

*Love,*
*Jim*

## An Khe
## Unit Protocols (LRRP Rules)

This was a 'unit in formation,' that is, the unit was forming and establishing itself and a sense of identity/belonging was growing among its members.

Regarding field duty, which everyone in the unit was expected to understand since *everyone* in the unit went through our training and pulled at least one mission, there was/were several commandments that everyone knew and understood, even though they were never written down anywhere:

POWs – any team that managed to obtain a prisoner in the field would immediately dope up the prisoner with a half of a dose of a morphine Syrette, both for security purposes and manageability of the prisoner. (Initially, all teams carried five morphine syrettes in their team medic bag. This was a controlled unit item, which was issued to the team after the mission alert.)

Contact, with POW – if a team had captured a POW and then engaged later in a fresh contact with the enemy (i.e., a shooting contact), the team's physical well being and safety were paramount, so the POW was to be slain immediately on the spot. This was necessary to increase the team's survival chances during the engagement with the enemy. The task/responsibility would fall on a pre-designated team member, normally the ATL, if possible. If not, the team member nearest the POW at the time of contact would execute him. (This was always mentioned in the oral five paragraph field order that the entire team participated in prior to deployment – it was just never written down, for obvious reasons!)

A contact was defined just as the word implied – contact with the enemy. This was to be avoided whenever possible, for two distinct reasons. The most obvious was the simple fact that our small number, and the distance from any friendly unit that usually necessitated our mission in the first place, did not seem adequate to engage in a shooting conflict with the enemy. We usually countered this shortcoming by packing heavy with weapons and ammo for our number of personnel.

The second was that our main goal was the gathering of surreptitious intelligence, and this we could not do while the enemy forces knew of our presence.

Contact, as defined above, did not necessarily mean that the firing of weapons was involved. Contact could also mean that the enemy had observed us, whether we tried to elude or not. Here the damage would already be done, for if the enemy was aware of our presence, our presence, and the mission's goal, was considered to be compromised, and the team would then be hurriedly extracted from the area. LRRPs, according to HQs, were considered too valuable to waste by leaving them in the field in a security-compromised situation.

The extracted team would then shame-facedly have to explain to the rest of us just how and why they had to be pulled, and could not complete their mission. This was considered to be the ultimate disgrace to us LRRPs – to be spotted in the field and subsequently withdrawn. To be 'shot out' of an area was one thing, but to be pulled out because they did not hide well enough was another matter altogether. Call it LRRP pride!

# Chapter Five

## My Very First Mission

This was my first time in the field, as an infantryman, and in tiger fatigues, albeit as a LRRP, yet!

Don't really remember much about this mission mechanically but this was significant in my development as it demonstrated the effects of concepts and mind-sets, and their impacts, both personally and to the "team". (This 'team concept' would be of paramount importance in all of my future LRRP activities.)

The team-leader was an *older* (at least 35) E-6 from a line company, so he was thoroughly imbued with the 'book principles' of infantry operations. That is, he knew how to operate in the Army way, and any other method(s) just did not measure up or else he would of known of them by now. Plus he only had about 40 days left in-country so he wasn't going to take any chances.

Anyhow, I remember us walking in the classic file configuration –front scout first, then the team leader, radioman or RTO (me), followed by the medic, assistant team leader, and finally the rear scout. We were in an area of really dense undergrowth and the going was slow, and somewhat noisy to my way of thinking. Like I already mentioned, this team leader wasn't about to take any chances and he had switched places with the ass't. team leader so he was now fifth in file - where the trail had already been broken in by the four men to his front.

I was exceedingly new to all of this, for all of my nine to ten months in-country so far had been as a radio-operator in an engineer battalion and this was my first chance to play as a soldier for real, so I had lots of questions and curiosity. But I also had the common sense to keep my mouth shut and just watch and learn. And I noticed a couple of things.

I knew where we were, if only because I had to call in our location coordinates and situation report twice a day. I called in exactly what the team leader told me to. And I'm pretty sure that the asst. team leader had an idea of where we were because he and the team leader talked together a couple of times. But the other three men had no idea as to where we were. The team leader was 'old Army' to the point that he didn't feel it necessary to share this info with everyone on the team. Some twisted sense of 'command prerogative,' I believe. Anyway, I personally made it a point to quietly inform the others every chance I got. Remember that I was young and naïve, and took to heart the training dictum that we were only a five to six man team, and *everyone* had to share *everything*, for the good of the team. And my imagination kept picturing us splitting up in the jungle, with not everyone knowing where we were and, consequently, not knowing where to go.

The other focal point of this training mission in my memory is a patch of elephant grass...

We were following a certain azimuth on the compass and I remember clearly that the team leader would not let the front scout make any detours to allow for terrain and natural obstacles. In other words, we had been traveling in as nearly a straight line as possible through the jungle as the old team leader kept us on course. And I *distinctly* remember it being emphasized in our training classes that we **never, ever** travel in a straight line, since if we were being observed it wouldn't be hard for the enemy to figure out just where we were headed and arrange a nasty surprise for us when we got there.

We arrived at what looked like a break in the trees, and encountered an area overgrown with ten to twelve feet tall elephant grass. This stuff is just what the name implies – a variety of giant grass, not bamboo that grows thickly together and reaches an amazing height. The individual blades of grass can be two to three inches wide, ten to twelve inches tall, and sharp as razor blades. The term "grass cuts" took on an entirely new dimension here in the jungle. One's hands and forearms would be cut and scratched as if you had been playing in a blackberry patch after trying to walk through just a few feet of elephant grass.

Anyhow, the azimuth we were following pointed dead ahead through the elephant grass, and that's precisely where we went. Once we were about eight feet into the grass we lost sight of where we had come from, the grass was that dense. And it takes a certain style of walking to navigate through elephant grass. You don't step normally; or else your legs would get fouled like a ship's propeller in heavy seaweed, by the long blades of grass. You have to shift your weight onto one leg, extend your other leg forward at an angle to your direction of travel, hook as many blades of grass as possible with this leg and then sweep them sideways. If done correctly, there is now a clump of grass blades swept to the side, held in place by your free leg. Now stand on this free leg, step up and forward with your other leg and repeat as before but now into the other direction, be it either left or right. In effect you are using your legs to bat the grass sideways out of your way, much as you do with your arms and hands for branches and leaves.

The drawback to this mode of travel, aside from the obviously physically demanding and tiring aspect, is the simple truth that you are walking blind as you do this. In thick elephant grass your visual depth is only three or four feet. Plus it is extremely noisy. After about 30 min to travel only about 50 feet, the team leader ordered everyone to take a turn on point here. Everyone except him! For he felt that he had to control the team. Each one of us also made the suggestion that we go around this grassy area and resume our line of march on the other side of this clearing. But he wouldn't have any of this. This is where the compass says to go, and this is where we're going!

He was only relying on what he knew that worked. But he was an ideal negative example as for trying new things. And remember, it was hammered into us that the enemy knew how the Army operated and reacted. And the enemy would react accordingly. That got my attention.

**Another Mission**

In hindsight, another safe training mission.

By this time, the older E-6 team leader was no longer in the unit. There were a handful of complaints and questions about his performance as a team leader in a new unit such as this, and one day we woke up and he was gone. We don't know if he rotated out of country back to the States or if he was sent back to his old line unit. He was gone, and that was all that mattered.

My new team leader was a Sgt. Cumba, the asst. team leader from the previously mentioned incident. I was now acting in the dual role of his asst team leader and as his RTO for a five man team.

Again team coherence and unity comes into play in this memory.

We had run out of water, in a dry AO, and still had another two days left in the mission so we were forced to call in for a water re-supply drop. These weren't recommended, but were available if necessary. Anytime we had to be re-supplied by chopper it was second nature to figure that the team's location had been pointed out and therefore compromised.

To minimize the possibilities of team location giveaways, water drops were done as the helicopter flew over the team's location without stopping or slowing down, thereby changing the chopper engine's pitch or RPMs, a dead giveaway to one who was listening_in a jungle in which one couldn't see. The water was actually contained in a long five gallon 'balloon' which was also inside several other five gallon balloons. This multi-layer effect of plastic envelopes protected the inner water-containing balloon from being punctured by thorns or branches as it tumbled through the forest canopy to the jungle floor. The only drawback occurred if the limply flexible giant frankfurter-like balloon got suspended in the forks of trees or branches above ground.

Four of our five man team were out of water. We had to 1) work on our water discipline in the future and 2) not rely so much on maps that indicated water should not be a problem in a given area. This was also my first experience with personal selfishness conflicting with the needs of the team: for one man, named T______ was the only one who had any water left and he *would not share it*, an action that was both foreign and inexcusable to me in my formative rookie phase.

In any event, the helicopter finally came on station and I was given the challenge, as the RTO, of directing it both to and over our location simply by listening to the engines as it flew around and giving it directions accordingly. As it was to fly over a small break in the trees at our location we were all prepared on the ground to flash our brightly covered red and yellow signal panels to the crew to indicate our position as 'friendlies.'

The helicopter flew directly over our position without seeing us, so I directed it out and around for another fly-over. This time they were looking for us, and when the chopper flew over the clearing the itchy-fingered door-gunner opened up on us as soon as he saw individuals on the ground. He wasn't waiting to ID some frantically waving colored pieces of cloth in the bushes – he saw some figures on the ground and opened up with his M-60. As Sgt. Cumba and I were laying on the ground we watched as a stream of bullets stitched up the ground and went right between us, parallel to our bodies, just like in the movies when they depict a close call in a battle scene!

We finally managed to calm down the flight crew and the water balloons were kicked out on the next pass. Four balloons were kicked out and we managed to retrieve three of them, salvaging enough water to last us for the next two days, with more effort put into our water discipline from that point on.

I never again asked for a water re-supply.

### Another Mission

Team leader – Sgt. Cumba

This one I remember as an observation mission. We were supposed to keep an eye on a coastal village way south of Bong Son and I believe south east of LZ Uplift, near the southern reaches of the Bong Son plain. This village was suspected of enemy activity or assistance and we were to monitor the comings and goings of individuals and groups from the highland region to the west, or inland.

All in all, a quiet lazy mission, with a minimum of movement on our team's part – we were supposed to remain hidden and unobserved on a ridge to the southwest of the village and watch and record all nighttime visitors from the hills.

Our procedure was to keep a couple of guys watching the village through binoculars, with another couple of guys casually observing all around us to prevent anybody from stumbling into our hiding spot. If you weren't watching somewhere, you could sleep. These were the kind of missions that every team wanted to pull!

Anyhow, I was dozing in the late morning, laying comfortably in the grasses in our spot. I was awakened by a nudging on my leg. This was not abnormal, for it was our habit to waken a teammate by nudging him with a stick, or a rifle barrel, to minimize our movement in our camping spot.

I woke slowly, somewhat groggily, and looked around me. There was no one trying to wake me up, and I started to wonder who was playing games with me. Then I felt another nudging, on my other leg, and I propped myself up on my elbows to look.

There, walking across my knee, just like crossing a log, was a large 5" spider! It had crossed over my other leg (the first 'nudging') and continued in the same direction across my other leg. I sleepily watched it crawl off my leg and disappear into the grass, laid down and went back to sleep.

And now, years later, I ask myself how I did that!

# Chapter Six

## Bong Son

With the advantage of maturity and hindsight I realize that my time spent in Bong Son (LZ English) as a LRRP was instrumental to my eventual good fortune as a team leader. For the majority of my stay here was as the LRRP RTO in the 1st Brigade's TOC, or Tactical Operations Center.

Whenever a team was fielded anywhere in the 1st Brigade's Area of Operations or AO, it was our policy to maintain an RTO in the HQ's 24 hours a day for as long as the team was in the field. Even though the teams were provided with all of the pertinent frequencies that they would need of all the various units (i.e., artillery, aviation units, infantry QRF) they were to call in sit-reps twice a day at pre-arranged times on our unit freq. Using our special codes many other RTO's would not know that breaking squelch once signified yes, twice meant no and three times meant I don't know. And if a team was either in contact or in a position where they could not talk by voice, our LRRP RTO's could, by asking the right questions, find out from the team exactly what was what out there. Plus, many times a team would call in only by breaking squelch and a non-LRRP RTO would have missed it. Also, in the middle of a contact is no time for the RTO to try and figure out our unit codes!

At the time I felt that I was just marking time with Commo duty, that it was keeping me dry in the monsoons, but that it was keeping me off field duty as a team-member. I know that the various team leaders were glad that I was on the radio whenever they had to call in, but at the time I didn't see it from their perspective. I just wanted to be back on a team!

This was my second time back in the Bong Son area, and at LZ English, but this time as a LRRP I was aware of so much more. When I was with the 8th Engineer Battalion we were pretty much restricted to the company area and hardly ever got outside the barbed wire perimeter. But as a LRRP we would be 'downtown' in the village whenever we didn't have to pull duty, and would occasionally fly out to various LZ's and firebases to coordinate for upcoming missions. And by seeing the tactical maps in the war room I began to realize just how extensive were the Bong Son plains and how rugged the surrounding highlands. (The plain had strategic importance because it was a major source of rice production.)

Plus, by being on radio watch in the HQ's 'war room' I would listen and get the feel for how the infantry units were waging their various battles throughout the AO. As a result of this sneak peek at the Brigade's workings in their inner sanctum I got a real good feel for how the game of war was played by an Airmobile unit – to wit, an initial sighting or contact, development of same, use of troops or artillery, use of helicopter resources, and follow-up.

Not only did I know what was going on out in the field with our teams because I had experience, but I also got to see how their reports were received and handled by the higher ups 'back at rear.' Not to mention all of the hoop-jumping that certain protocols warranted, and a fairly new concept to a young one like me called 'prioritization.' Knowing full well how things were handled in the rear helped me immensely later on when I had to call in reports of my own, for I had an understanding of how they'd be received and worded them accordingly whenever I had the presence of mind to do so.

## Fun

Our living compound at LZ English consisted of three GP-Medium tents for the troops and one GP-Small that served as our Orderly Room in the front half and our Lt.'s sleeping quarters in the rear.

Below us were another couple of GP tents and a bunch of dog kennels, for this is where the Scout Dog Platoon had their living area when their teams were back at the rear. Two oddball units that hung out together, only because the head honchos felt us to be different, so they lumped us together. In any case, it worked and we all got along well, and even had some cookouts together.

We thought the Scout Dogs were crazy and suicidal, for their job was to have a dog and its handler walk point for a line unit as they conducted their operations, be it in a built-up area or out in the jungle. The dog and handler were trained to find booby-traps, mines and provide early warning of an impending ambush. Walking in front of a noisy line unit struck us LRRPs as downright crazy.

They, in turn, felt that we were the crazy ones going out alone with only five or six men total. They felt, honestly, that there was safety in numbers. And they liked the idea that an entire infantry company was right behind them. It was all in one's point of view, I guess.

Anyhow, one afternoon some of the stray chickens that seemed indigenous to the Bong Son area strayed into our compound. I remember a total of four birds clucking in between the tents. Somebody got the idea of a BBQ and the chase was on.

As I recall it, four birds were being chased by about seven LRRPs. The birds were squawking, everyone was laughing and shouting, and generally getting in each other's way. It was very reminiscent of a bunch of youths trying to catch a greased pig at the county fair. The fact that the chickens were sober and the LRRPs were not did not seem important at the time.

Two of our tents were knocked down when the guy ropes were dislodged by careening bodies. It all seemed worth it when ONE chicken was finally cornered and caught amid a raining flurry of loose feathers.

Having alcohol in their system, the hunters could not wait for a proper BBQ and some bozo got the brilliant idea of cooking the bird with C-4! After all, it boiled water, didn't it?

The end result was a charred carcass smelling of burned feathers and a bunch of shame-faced guys struggling to re-erect their tents before the officers found out about their 'hunt'.

**Hypocrisy**

Pacification – the process of "winning the hearts and minds" of the Vietnamese populace to 'our' anti-Communist way of thinking.

While we were at LZ English I had a 'girlfriend' downtown who ran a laundry just outside the main gate, and her sister ran the brothel next door. So guess where all of the LRRPs hung out downtown? There was no theft or missing tiger fatigues, either, which happened a lot at the other local laundries. Our tiger fatigues were important to us and hard to get, since we bought them on the local market back at An Khe. Preferably at the Montagnard village. These were more durable than those offered at Vietnamese stalls. Plus they were 'black' camouflaged, and not a dark blue.

The girlfriend's name was Hai; she had a two-year old son, and was supposedly married to an ARVN captain stationed in Saigon. She was very personable and all of the LRRPs got along well with her.

I was gone for awhile, either on a mission, or R&R, or whatever. When I got back this story was related to me by Sgt. Wyman Smith.

Hai got sick. Really, really sick and the other guys were worried about her. So Smitty and a couple of the others brought her onto LZ English to have a doctor take a look at her.

Trouble was, the MPs would not let her onto the base, even though it was obvious that she was truly sick. The official policy was that all locals had to go to a clinic down in the town of Bong Son proper, several miles away.

This kind of ticked off the LRRPs, who were genuinely concerned for her. They ended up 'borrowing' (stealing) a field ambulance and driving her to a New Zealander outpost just a couple of miles up the road in the opposite direction. There the doctor at the clinic gave her an exam, and some antibiotics.

She was all better by the time I got back. And from that point on we all got *remarkably* good service at both local establishments downtown. As long as we were in tiger fatigues, anyway, to identify us to the locals who worked there!

**Vietnamese Betrayal or American Naivete/Arrogance?**

The Brigade TOC was located in an old French plaster-and-brick church located on a small gentle hillock near the SW end of LZ English. It was surrounded by a security fence comprised of several coils of barbed concertina wire to a height of five feet and a depth of about eight feet. The main entrance to the compound was a wire gate manned continuously by at least two armed guards at the base of the hill, 100 feet from the church building.

A dirt road was the only access to the main gate.

As you approached the TOC, via the road, the LRRP living compound was on the left side of the road about 150 meters from the main gate, with the Scout Dog Platoon located below them. Fifty meters further on, closer to the TOC, was the HQs barbershop, staffed by Vietnamese locals who had passed the necessary personal investigations and background checks. Seventy-five meters from the gate, and down to the left in a hollow, was the Military Intelligence's office and headquarters. They had a close coordination and working rapport with the civil authorities, so it was not unusual to see Vietnamese of all sorts this close to the TOC.

As I remember it, on the right side of the access road was higher ground with better drainage and runoff, a high-demand characteristic during the monsoon season. On the right side of the road were situated the staff officers' quarters and various communication elements with electronic equipment and a forest of antennas.

Behind the TOC at the top of the hill proper, in what looked like used to be something akin to an orchard was situated the helicopter pad, which was large enough to occasionally accommodate the twin-rotor CH-47. This area also contained the TOC's requisite generators and POL (Petroleum and Oil, Liquids) point.

To the immediate south of LZ English was an expanse of rice paddies and growing fields, which comprised the bulk of the Bong Son plain. Several miles to the south was the town proper of Bong Son, at the crossroads of the Bong Son River, Highway QL-1, and the blown bridge, of French construction, where the national railroad crossed the river.

All in all, a very tidy, efficient and secure layout for a HQs area.

I don't remember the exact date, but it was during my stint as an RTO in the TOC. LZ English suffered another periodic nighttime mortar attack, accompanied by a half-hearted ground- force probe. (I do know that I had been on duty there for a couple of months at least.) The resulting mortar damage was minimal, and four or five enemy bodies were found in the outer green-line wire afterwards.

Several days after this attack the word was all over LZ English – one of the bodies found in the wire had been identified as the barber, hired to work in the HQs barbershop, right in the intelligence hub of the entire LZ! So much for thorough background checks, either by our people or the locals.

### RTO Incident

Barney's team (SSG Barnes) was out in the field and I was pulling night-time RTO duty in the TOC. Our radio was set up near the rear of the TOC, right next to the radios of the 1/9th the 1st Squadron of the 9th Cavalry Regiment. There were three aerial Troops in the Squadron' Alpha, Bravo and Charlie, and a fourth jeep mounted unit called Delta Troop that served the Cav.

They were the combination reconnaissance aviation/infantry/ mounted infantry unit that usually provided the ships for our insertions, aerial recons, and gun-ships when we had a contact. Each of the separate troops had a platoon of infantry known as 'the Blues' that also were our usual QRF (Quick Reaction Force) that was the first unit to respond when we were in trouble. As a result of their working so closely with us a camaraderie had developed between us and I became friendly with their RTO's.

The TOC was set up in an old French church and we were set up near the rear. Towards the front of the church, where the crucifix should have been was a huge war map just like we had seen in the movies. This was primarily the Cav's TAOR (Tactical Area of Responsibility) – the Bong Son Plain and the surrounding highlands. But this map also showed the coastline to our east (and how close we were to the South China Sea) and a good portion of II Corps.

The first major valley to our west, the beginning of the highlands, was the An Lao Valley. This was notorious as a VC stronghold and any unit that was deployed there usually had a contact. These contacts were normally with larger units, and not the minor two to three individuals that were more frequent throughout Viet Nam up to this point.

The middle of the TOC consisted of a large sandtable mounted on what appeared to be a couple of Ping-Pong tables on sawhorses. This sandtable depicted, in miniature representation, the entire Cav AO from the larger war map. The various units that comprised the 1st Brigade had their stations of VR/C-524 radios and RTO's set up along the two lengthy walls of the church building and the 'altar area' was the working area and tables of the Brigade Commander and the duty officers. This, then, was the immediate nerve center of the U.S. Army for about 50 miles in any direction from here.

Barney was out in the field, and had been for a couple of days. He was pulling an observation mission on one of the higher ridges at the mouth of the An Lao Valley, acting both as an early warning system to all 'friendlies' in the area if he spotted any movements and also to report to HQs if he noticed anything unusual happening in the valley. This valley had had all of its inhabitants relocated and had been declared a free-fire zone, that is, any people observed within the valley had no business being there and were subject to being shot on sight by the allied forces.

It was well after midnight and the only people in the TOC were myself, the 1/9th RTO (a young E-6 who was pulling radio duty after a tour as a helicopter crew chief) and a couple of other RTO's along the far wall. The duty officer was nowhere in sight. All in all, it was a deserted HQs.

To make a long story short, Barney's OP, Observation Post, site had movement all around him and he was in shooting contact with an unknown number of enemy. There was no one around for me to report to, and I didn't want to leave the radio to wake our Lt. (Lt. Utter, if I remember correctly) in our quarters area (tent), or waste time trying to track down the duty officer.

I asked Barney all of the requisite questions to prepare a sit-rep, and got the feeling that he wanted out of there. The 1/9th RTO was right next to me listening interestedly (and knowingly) to my exchange with Barney and said that he could get the standby bird cranked in three minutes. I told him to go ahead, just in case.

I kept talking with Barney and it was getting worse out there where he was, and still we were pretty much alone in the TOC. I asked him if he requested extraction and his reply was "Get me the fuck out of here!" (I took that as a 'Yes.')

By now the standby bird was cranked up, the crew was ready to take-off and still no duty officer. So I told the other RTO to go ahead and send the bird out to pick up Barney's team. That bird, and gunship escorts, were immediately enroute to Barney's location. For all practical purposes an E-6 (the other RTO) and an E-5 (me) were in charge of the Army, as far as Barney and the helicopters were concerned. I had no authorization to withdraw a team from their mission, and he had no permission to commit Aircraft like he did. But it needed to be done.

The helicopter with Barney's team landed about 45 minutes later at the TOC's helipad and then all hell seemed to break loose. The duty officer magically appeared and demanded to know what was going on, so I told him. His face looked kind of shocked as I recounted the sequence of events that happened during his absence.

A couple of hours later the Brigade Commander had my heels locked as he gave me a real polite dressing down, to the effect that he could not run an orderly operation as long as things like this happened without his knowing about it, and that a LRRP team was supposed to stay in place until the tactical situation was thoroughly evaluated, and *then* a decision would be made as to whether to withdraw the team or to exploit the situation by sending in the assigned QRF unit that was supposedly on standby for the team in the field.

As the dressing down continued I almost felt sorry for him because I could understand his point of view. But deep down, as a LRRP, I really didn't care that much. All that seemed to matter to me was that Barney had requested extraction. And I got him out!

### Caliber of Individuals

This did not happen to me, but it's more than second-hand reporting, for I was the rear RTO on duty.

Again SSG Barnes was out in the field. I took a personal interest in his sit-reps because my close buddy SGT Burt Penkunis was on his team. He was the second oldest guy (25 years) in the 1st Platoon and had kind of adopted me like a younger brother. To me he was also experienced in the ways of the military since he had already completed a tour of duty in Germany, hence his SGT E-5 status. He was Barney's RTO, was happy with that assignment, and refused the responsibility of either the TL or ATL positions. Whenever Barney's team was back at the rear Penkunis and I were physically together as if we were chained.

Barney's team medic was an authentic school-trained medic, Sp/5 John Dempsey. He had been with a line unit and was sent to us to get him out of that unit. It seems that his company had come under heavy fire from a village in an operation and all of its leadership command had either been killed or incapacitated. Doc Dempsey then found himself with the radio and he had called in one of the Cav's two CH-47 gunships, either Birth Control or Guns-a-Go-Go, and wasted the entire village. He saved his unit, the incoming firing stopped, but the resultant publicity made for bad press, so he was re-assigned to us. He was a damn good medic and field trooper.

Barney's team had had another contact, again on the high edges of the An Lao valley, which was a 'hot' free-fire zone. A 'free-fire zone' was an area that had been de-populated for the benefit of the military, by having all of the inhabitants re-located to a safer area under 'government control'. Lock, stock and barrel, the entire population was moved, sometimes forcibly, with only the possessions that they could carry. Individual homes, and villages, were essentially abandoned for the needs of politics and the exigencies of war. When one realizes that entire families had to abandon their ancestral fields, schools and cemeteries to live in virtual refugee shanty-town conditions, its not surprising that the civilian population was not entirely swayed to our way of thinking and required 'pacification'.

The resultant abandoned geography was then declared a free-fire zone, with no human habitation or activity authorized or permitted by the military forces. Any individuals who happened to be spotted by either aircraft or ground units were subject to being fired upon under a 'shoot on sight' standing directive. Whether they were armed or not.

Barney's team, as stated, was in another contact, a shooting contact, in the rocky and bouldered area on the side of the valley, and was eventually extracted, under fire.

When they got back, Burt showed us where his heel had been shot off of the sole of his left boot, and one of his canteens had been shot off of his rucksack.

After the de-briefing, we heard from Barney as to what Dempsey had done.

The team was surrounded in a rocky area, much like in the old Westerns of the movies. One of the enemy threw a Chi-com hand grenade (like the older German 'potato masher') into their position, and Dempsey, being closest, jumped on it. It was a dud, did not go off, and Dempsey and Barney locked eyes and shared a grim smile that only they could understand. Not more than five minutes later another hand grenade landed in their midst, and again Dempsey instinctively threw himself upon it. This one again did not go off, but for a different reason – this was an American hand grenade, but the excitable enemy on the other side of the rocks forgot to pull the pin to arm it! Dempsey then pulled the pin himself and 'returned it to sender' by heaving it back towards the enemy. This time it went off.

Afterwards, back in the rear, Dempsey maintained that he had made no conscious decision to jump on either grenade. Being the closest, both times, he just found himself lying on the grenades by the time he could ask himself *'What am I doing here?'*

Dempsey was never put in for a medal for his actions, because our unit did not give out medals. They would be unwanted publicity for a unit that was trying to remain unknown.

# Chapter Seven

## R&R Attack

And so the 1st Cav was moving again, only this time it was a Move! All the way up to the DMZ we had heard, this time to help the Marines. Nobody seemed to know anything definite, but gossip was everywhere. We finally got the word that we were indeed moving north into I Corps area, and would eventually end up around Dong Ha, just south of the Marines' AO, yet still we would be the furthest northern Army unit.

It was decided that about half of the unit would fly up as part of the quartering party, to secure our final destination areas and begin to set up our quarters. My buddy Burt and I considered ourselves fortunate to remain behind and go up in convoy with our vehicles and equipment. We considered this a prelude to our upcoming R&R in Hong Kong, for we would arrive up north just two days before we had to turn around and head for Cam Ranh Bay to begin our R&R.

But the Army threw a curve at us, for we had to load up all our stay-behind company equipment and then all of the remaining Cav units would drive overland in convoy to Qui Nhon, where we were supposed to load onto Army boats and sail up to the Marine base at Da Nang.

Army boats? No one, not even the officers, knew that the Army had boats!

And that's just what we did. We drove all day, riding on top of our stolen 2 ½ ton truck, and arrived in Qui Nhon around midnight. We couldn't begin loading onto the mysterious boats until later in the afternoon, so we were ordered to remain with the vehicles and guard the gear until then. And as soon as anyone in charge turned their backs, half of our contingent promptly took off and headed downtown to get drunk and/or get laid. (The prevalent rationale operating here was that that was our job – *to sneak around and not get caught!*)

When all of our equipment was finally on-loaded onto some rusting hulks that even Tugboat Annie would refuse to crew on, Burt and I, and a couple of others, decided to sleep on the deck at the bow, rather than ride with the vehicles down below decks. I may not have had a college education like the officers but even I knew these boats were made of steel and iron, (the rust was proof of that), and steel does not float very well.

After three days sailing up the coast and learning that the boats were actually manned by Army sailors (one of the better-kept secrets of the entire war) we landed at Da Nang and began to off-load. And here we got into our first run-in with the Marine mentality. The powers that be, in charge of the Marines, did not want any Army versus Marine trouble, so we were kept off base. But they also didn't want us low-life army types to go exploring downtown either, so some dimwit ordered all the vehicles parked alongside the base's wire enclosure, yet outside of it.

This really didn't sit well with any of us, and our vehicles were parked right outside the maintenance and repair facility for all of the Marine tanks, self-propelled howitzers, search-light tanks, and other armored vehicles. As the evening wore on some of us began drinking and grumbling, in that order. Eventually one of the more sober of us began to notice the sentry as he made his rounds on the far side of the repair yard, and remarked that the sentry must be new in country, or stupid, because he had established a routine to his beat that anyone could penetrate. Sober or drunk, the same idea hit all of us within one minute of his remark.

Now our truck was parked about two feet from the wire fence, alongside of it and the top of our equipment was at least two feet above the razor-wire atop the wire fence. After a quick self-generating frag order agreed to by all personnel present, half of our group began to create a hole in the middle of the stored and carefully packed equipment, while the other half, after making sure that the sentry had just left, jumped from the truck over the fence, and into the yard. We now had about 20 minutes to go exploring/shopping.

Now remember, we were infantry, and had no idea what kind of vehicles these were, but we were over them and into them like kids on monkey bars at the playground. And when we realized that the ten-station pre-set crystalline radios were not bolted into the vehicles but would slide out by loosening a simple wing nut, the shopping spree was on with a vengeance. One of us would finagle a way into a vehicle and get the radio out, hand it to two guys waiting on the ground, who would then run it to the fence and hand it over to the truck crew, who would then bury it in the hole in our gear.

We ended up with seven radios, to use as bartering goods later, and would have got twice as many were it not for Burt. He had spent a tour in Germany, and was somewhat familiar with heavy machinery. While we were handing contraband over the fence, we were dismayed to hear one of the tanks fire itself up and our stomachs turned cold when we saw the turret begin to swing around. Burt, very drunk, was not shopping – he was playing. This ended our shopping trip, as we ran to the active tank and hauled his ass out of there and over the fence before the sentry returned. His only comment was that he was pissed that the turret was not armed, for he wanted to blow the guard shack and maintenance office.

The next morning we drove north, our group ending up at an old crumbling French fort just outside the town of Quang Tri. Our new home was designated LZ Betty, and the bulk of the other Cav units with us were lodged at the larger LZ Sharon a quarter-mile away. We were lodged in the NW corner of the perimeter, downwind of Sharon's dumpsite. (We found out it was downwind whenever Sharon's green-line troops used tear gas to clear the dumpsite of foraging civilians).

Burt and I spent the night there and in the morning were to hitch a ride to the airfield at Hue/Phu-Bai, and from there catch a military hop back to An Khe for our R&R. We left all of our gear and weapons there for teammates to use, as they were settling into a new area and did not know what to expect. So we traveled with a change of clothes, a carton of cigarettes and a pistol, each of us.

We had a six hour wait at the Phu Bai airfield, and spent the time bullshitting with an SF captain who was traveling with a full platoon of Montagnards, of the Bru tribe. We finally boarded a C-130 with nine others, heading to An Khe. The other nine passengers looked strange to us and it took me awhile to figure it out. They were obviously rear types, but it was their abundance of what Burt and I called 'baby-fat' that set them apart in our eyes. In any case Burt and I laid out on the closed cargo-ramp door to catch a nap rather than sit in the red nylon-webbing seats with the others.

About 20 minutes out from An Khe the plane's crew chief woke us and told us we were close. So we grabbed our waterproof bags and rubbed the sleep from our eyes. Then things began to get interesting. As the cobwebs finally cleared from our heads, we heard a loud ping, like a bolt popping, near us. Burt looked over and raised his eyebrows. Then we heard four or five more in quick succession as the plane began its descent. (We later discovered that at about this time the pilot was radioing the An Khe tower, telling them to get all those people off the runway 'cuz he was coming in on final. They responded that they had "no personnel on the runway at that time"!)

Extremely wary and edgy by now, Burt and I waited while the plane touched down and taxied to the off-load area. With the engines still running, the pilot opened the cockpit door and then the exit door on the left of the plane forward of the red-marked propeller line.

"Get out now," he yelled at us passengers. "We're under attack!" And then he was out the door followed by the crew chief and co-pilot.

The other nine seemed to take forever to exit the aircraft, but when Burt and I hit the tarmac outside we lost sight of them in the crowd, for there were people running around everywhere – but they weren't GI's, they were VC. Burt and I, apparently on the same mental wavelength, hit the ground together under the left wing – Burt facing to the rear, me facing forward, each of us with a pistol, observing up close and personal a VC attack against an army airfield. And through it all, the C-130's engines were still whining, the pilot not having completed his shutdown procedure.

Our plane was behind a CV-2 Caribou that was being loaded or unloaded by one guy on a forklift. I watched him dash out of the plane's cargo bay as mortars began falling all around us and scurry underneath the forklift to obtain overhead cover. While I was watching him, Burt was watching the short, pudgy pilot do some broken-field running in among the conex containers, dodging mortar-rounds all the while as he made his way to the airfield's op-center. Burt later said that he didn't think the pilot was going to make it, but somehow he did.

As the pilot was making his run, I watched as a mortar-round exploded on the safety screen above thc forklift operator's seat, and just knew that the guy underneath had had it. But I was wrong – I saw him squirm around some as if he was going to get up and run, but then he decided to stay there as the mortars were still falling. Smart choice on his part, even if his ears were ringing.

Burt and I talked with one another, covering one another. We were afraid to move, and we were both afraid to shoot – I had only five rounds in my .38 and he had only one magazine in his .45. We had left all our weapons and gear for the field teams to use up north, where the action was. We were going on R&R!

I watched as a naked pair of legs approached our plane from the right side, and worked their way forward to the nose of the aircraft. I kept my pistol on the guy but never really had a clear shot. I watched the legs stop at the nose gear and saw a burlap bag drop alongside the tires. "Satchel charge," I said to Burt, and we both covered our heads with our arms, as we laid there hiding behind laundry bags with clothes and cigarettes in them.

The legs ran away and the charge went off with a woomph! The nose-gear strut buckled and the nose of the aircraft hit the tarmac. *Dumb shit!* I remember thinking, for if the VC had placed the charge higher in the nose gear wheel-well he would really have destroyed the plane. But as it was the plane was not going anywhere for awhile.

After the pair of legs left, I started to look around farther out. Across the airstrip, where the green-line was closest to the town proper of An Khe I watched in horror as two of the guard towers were blown at their base, and crumpled to the ground. If the 173rd Airborne Brigade (moving into Camp Radcliffe now that the Cav was moving out) followed the same procedures, there were at least four GI's in each of those towers. Not any more, I thought, as I mentally recited a quick prayer for the dead. Then I watched in awe and admiration as the center tower between the two blown ones began to fire a steady stream of tracers straight down to the ground from 35 feet up. The GI manning the M-60 machine-gun was apparently walking around the edge of the tower platform shooting straight down as he did so, keeping the sappers on the ground away from the base of his tower, thereby preventing his from being blown. *When this is all over I want to shake that guy's hand,* I remember thinking.

Burt and I remained where we were for about one hour, until things quieted down, and then made our way to the op-center, where we talked for awhile with the shaken forklift operator. Not until the all-clear sirens began blowing to signal the official end of the attack did we venture out again to view the aftermath. By this time all the clerks and jerks in camp had been organized into clean-up details and were walking everywhere.

While we were still in the op-center Burt was talking to one GI in his undershorts. This guy had been sleeping in the GCA (ground control approach) shack out in the middle of the airstrip in the grassy areas between the runway and taxiway. He was awakened by all the commotion and shot two VC within five feet of his doorway as he stepped out and began sprinting to the op-center. With a shotgun, no less. He was kinda rattled as he talked to Burt, but that was highly understandable.

As we walked towards the GCA shack, surveying the damage, I heard Burt let loose with a string of profanity and anger that I had never heard from him in all the time that I'd known him. There, lying neatly in a row on the grass were 11 half-dressed bodies of Viet Cong attackers. They were all shirtless and wearing shorts – 4 of them wore sandals, the rest were barefoot. It took a lot of courage to attack a heavily-defended and manned airfield dressed like that, but I still wondered what it was that had set Burt off like that. He just looked at me with the coldest set of eyes that I had ever seen on a human and pointed at the bodies.

"Look at their heads," he managed to utter through a throat constricted with anger. I looked. And looked again. For not one of the 11 attackers that we were standing in front of had any ears left. The clean-up crews, who were not in the attack at all, had cut off all of their ears. As souvenirs. Right then I began to feel the same rage as Burt, and swore to myself that I'd never respect a REMF again.

We were both so enraged at this desecration that we just left, preferring to walk the 3 miles to our orderly room, to sign in for our R&R. It was a quiet walk, neither of us saying a word.

# Chapter Eight

## Quang Tri

This is the area where I spent the most time in one locale and as a result I actually developed a kinship with this area to the point where I felt physically comfortable and at ease here and truly came to identify with it as 'a home' in my memories. Also, this is where I seemed to pull the majority of my missions, all of them in the capacity of a team leader. It was here that I grew and matured, both as an individual and as a competent, confident LRRP.

On the map of Viet Nam we were located just outside the village/ hamlet of Quang Tri. On the military overlay we were the northern-most Army unit in I Corp, south of the U.S. Marines located at Dong Ha about six miles to our north. We took over from the Army's 5th Mech. Div. and were quartered at LZ Betty, which was originally an old French fort. By the time of our arrival it had crumbled to the point where it was simply a large square concrete enclosure, with several interior walls from the original rooms and billets still standing. No roofing had survived the passage of time. This became the location of the 1st Brigade TOC, the LRRPs, the Red Cross facility, the wash point and an infantry unit for perimeter security that always rotated the duty.

To our west about ½ mile was the sprawling complex of the 1st

Brigade proper – it's mainline units, support facilities, aviation units and all of the supplies required. This base was designated LZ Sharon.

The remainder of the 1st Cavalry Div, the 2nd and 3rd Brigades and all other units were quartered at Camp Evans approximately 20-30 miles to our south.

As to the LRRPs, this was the platoon (about four teams) that had been stationed at Bong Son (LZ English) to our south in II Corps. Plus we retained about five of our Montagnard scouts, the rest abandoning the Cav when it moved north. Their home was in the south and that's the only place that they wanted to fight. They would simply sign on with another American force in the area. Ours were somewhat mercenary, being paid the wages of a Vietnamese NCO, which amounted to about $50 -$75 per month. Recently the bulk of our missions had been quiet observation and surveillance, with little contact, and these scouts considered this easy duty. So they stayed with us for what they considered easy money.

Regardless, we were gratified that they were still with us. The Montagnards would only go to the field with people that *they* had confidence in, and I felt proud that I was one of the two team leaders that had these scouts assigned to their respective teams. Sgt. Parkinson was the other team leader.

And our good fortune continued, as to the nature of our missions. For the Cav had moved north prior to the Marine debacle at Khe Sanh, and the Cav's mission was to help stop the infiltration of the NVA through the DMZ to our north and from the Laotian highlands to our west. So far the Cav had been fighting primarily the Viet Cong, or guerilla forces, in the south and now we would be up against better-trained and better-equipped regular forces. As a result the vast majority of our missions in I Corps would be area recon and surveillance for enemy movement and routes, and their staging areas. In short, more missions where our contact with the enemy was to be discouraged, which was fine with us. For we kind of enjoyed the challenge of sneaking in and staying undetected – to the kid in all of us this was the ultimate game of hide and seek!

## Fun

Three of us snuck downtown into the main village one day without a pass, or the village had been declared off-limits, I really don't remember. But we weren't supposed to be there – that's the point. "We" consisted of SSG Carr, myself and my Montagnard scout Blol.

As I remember it, no sooner had we sat down at what amounted to (or passed for) a sidewalk café/bar and ordered a drink than we noticed some MP's had spotted us. We left the café/bar and started down the street and saw another MP jeep at the end of the street, intending to cut us off.

So we did the obvious – we cut through the backyard to the 'next block' to elude the MP's on the first street. As we entered the next street, there were more MPs waiting, apparently conducting a sweep, and these spotted us. So we took off running, the MPs in pursuit. By now there were four MP jeeps involved and it seemed there were a lot of solo MPs chasing us.

We were on our third or fourth alley/street when Blol obviously got tired of the game. He sat down at the next café as we rounded a corner and started to smile, with a twinkle in his eye.

He ordered a beer from the owner, looked at us and said "You American, me Vietnamese. You run. I sit and drink beer." He was right – the MPs would never pick him out from the customers since they were looking for American GIs only.

Later, back at camp, it was funny. But at the moment…

By the way – Carr and I were *not* caught. That would've been embarrassing!

## Monetary Policy

The economy of South Viet Nam was a shambles, and the black market was thriving. Unless one has seen a wartime economy and its disastrous effect all of the explanations in the world are just empty and sterile descriptive phrases.

Imagine, if you will, a rice farmer who toils throughout the growing season to produce enough rice crop to feed his family for the coming year and hopes to have enough surplus to sell at the market for manufactured necessities. He is lucky to earn a cash equivalent of $35 a month for his labors. But his wife and/or children can sell Coca-Cola to GIs for fifty cents a can! The cash necessary to operate on this black market enterprise negates his labors, essentially, yet they are necessary in order to eat.

As a result, and to lessen the impact of inflation U.S. greenbacks were outlawed in RVN, and were replaced with military scrip, or 'funny money' or 'monopoly money.' This and the Vietnamese piastre were the accepted forms of monetary exchange.

While we were stationed up north the first 'switching' or scrip conversion took place. In effect, the military issued a new form of MPC to combat hoarding and the devaluation of the piastre, more so than it was, anyway. This conversion took place simultaneously throughout all of South Viet Nam, with all U.S. forces confined to their bases for 48 hours to facilitate the exchange and provide some guarantee of security to the unannounced exchange.

When the change went into effect, the impact was horrendous on the local economies that were black-market dependent. This included a lot of local economies that had flourished just outside military camps. Overnight, people's fortunes were not just decimated, but wiped out. Once past the conversion hour, all previously issued military scrip was worthless – it could not be converted, even at a loss. The only exceptions were units that were deployed and did not have a chance to convert, and even then their paperwork requirements were daunting!

It was truly pathetic to see Vietnamese locals outside military installations with wicker baskets full of useless MPC, hoping to get some kind of conversion rate. It was also an eye-opener as to the extent that the hidden economy was operating in RVN.

## Attitudes

My Montagnard scout Blol was going home to Ban Me Thuot for a 30-day leave.

We all knew that he was low on cash (he really had no money) so

Sgt. Lee Hennings and I both offered to loan him some money. Like the rest of the Yards, Blol had a lot of pride, but both Lee and I were his friends so it was not an insult to him. We even thought that he would accept it from us.

We were surprised when he said no. We even tried to reason with him to take it, since the transportation system in RVN was haphazard at best.

He said, "No sweat. If I need money, I buku cowboy Vietnamese!"

In other words, if he needed money he would holdup and rob a Lambretta full of Vietnamese civilians, just like a highway bandit. Remember, there was no love lost between the Vietnamese and the Montagnard peoples.

### Peers

As I was returning back to the unit after a 30-day extension leave, I had to pass through the company HQs at Camp Evans before reporting to the 1st Platoon up at LZ Betty and rejoining my team.

The new First Sergeant there drafted me as a front scout to complete a team for a mission. Out of two platoons at Camp Evans there were too many sick calls and individuals riding the roster to flesh out one team. He called a company formation and really downgraded everyone there for his having to use a team-leader (me) to fill out a team.

This new team leader was notorious for making contact, and bragged that all he needed in the field was "bullets and water." On the mission, we heard movement below us on a hillside. He never waited to find out if it was animal or human, but had me throw a couple of hand grenades over the edge of the hill as the team vacated the area in a hurry.

So he had another 'contact' to his credit – and I still to this day don't think that humans made the noises that we heard.

My big fear, what scared me the most, was the idea that the company might keep me at Camp Evans with a bunch of strangers that I didn't know, and of whom I definitely had no faith in after that particular fiasco.

But they did send me back to LZ Betty, if only because I worked with the Montagnards and they with me. I was *very* glad to get back to people, and an area, that I knew and felt comfortable with.

To further illustrate my unease mentioned in the last two paragraphs above, this incident or memory fragment happened as I was passing through Camp Evans for an R&R, a leave, or whatever.

I only remember that I was at Camp Evans for a short time, catching military flights either north or south. What's important is that I was only passing through, and looked in on a friend of mine, Mac (SGT Dave McWilliams) who relayed this story to me.

We were bullshitting and catching up on gossip and he said that this place (Camp Evans) was really fucked up and that I was lucky to still be at LZ Betty. Not only were there too many new guys in the unit, but the unit was turning to shit. I naturally asked what he meant, and he said that he didn't think the new Commanding Officer was worth a damn.'

When I asked him to explain, because this affected everyone, regardless of where we were stationed, he replied that they had a team in contact the other week. The CO was in his hootch reading a paperback western novel. When someone from the Commo center went and told him that a team was in the shit, he answered that they should let him know how it turned out!

He never went to the HQs, never even left his cot! The NCOIC, SSG Barnes was in charge during the entire event. This was more than shocking, frustrating, and very scary to us field troops.

We at LZ Betty had never met the new Commanding Officer, just got word that we had a new CO at Camp Evans. Mac related that he was a West Point graduate, and that after he got his education and commission he planned on leaving the army. He didn't care for the military, but was stuck in the Army for five years, and was just marking time. And we got him as our CO.

Mac had nothing good to say about him, and his impact on the unit was obvious, as indicated by the previous incident above. And the caliber of new recruits was lower, at least to us older LRRPs, by the amount of drugs and alcohol, and sick calls that were in evidence at Camp Evans.

# Chapter Nine

## Another Mission

Don't remember the specific mission objective, but it was probably another area recon job.

We were camped on the forward slope of a high finger of land that stopped abruptly at the edge of a large river that flowed down from the Laotian hills to our west to the seacoast at the eastern edge of Quang Tri. We had been there overnight, in a blustery monsoon, and had been watching the river as an infiltration route. Our camp was about 150' above the surface of the water.

During the late afternoon and into the early evening we had heard voices just below us, where a smaller stream flowed into the larger river. We even heard a couple of feminine voices laughing, leading us to believe that there was some sort of rest area encampment being utilized just below us. Due to the reduced visibility and bad weather we had no visual confirmation, just the continuous sound of voices. They made no attempt to keep quiet so we figured that we were safe and unnoticed.

The decision was made to call in artillery on the rest area, and it took me two or three marking rounds before I fired for effect. I remember crouching down over the radio and being adjusted in my arty fire by Lee Hennings, a 6' 2" black man (he was my Montagnard 'blood-brother,' along with Blol) who was looking straight down onto the encampment area from the crotch of a tree eight feet off the ground. When I fired for effect, they were right on target and Lee was so excited that he dropped from the tree and began hopping up and down on the ground. By this time I had become 'clinically detached' while I was concentrating on my task on the radio, but I do remember the very unusual image of my asst team leader 'bouncing in the woods.' I guess in the woods, in the rain, one would blow it out where one could!

The weather stayed shitty for the rest of the mission and we were lucky to be airlifted out of that area as it was. There was no air mission possible to assess the outcome of the artillery barrage, so I'll never know the results. But we did not hear any more voices below us.

**Another Mission**

We had just been dropped into the brush at last light, or roughly ½ hour before total dark in the deceptively gentle-appearing foothills at the beginning of the western highlands. From the air it appeared to be gently sloping and rolling terrain, but on the ground under the triple canopy it was truly rugged going more often than not.

Anyhow, we had just been inserted, moved a short distance off the LZ and had 'gone to ground' for a commo check with both the insertion bird and our base at the rear. It was our practice to establish commo immediately after insertion, for obvious reasons, while we still had the aircraft in the area and for us to lay quiet for 15 to 20 minutes to see if our insertion had been detected by the other side. Occasionally we would also get the unwelcome news from the inserting aircraft that we had missed the intended LZ, and they would give us our real location. Good-to-know stuff!

Just the same, we were all laying low on the ground and I had just established radio contact with our aircraft orbiting high and off in the distance so as not to draw any undue attention to our area. I had made the initial call to our home base when I heard a cry of pain from "Little LRRP," one of the shortest individuals to be accepted into the

U.S. Army. He did not meet the minimum height requirement and had to get a special waiver to enlist. Sad to say, I do not remember his real name, just that we called him "Little LRRP" due to his height, or lack of it.

He was laying on the ground directly behind me, and as he was laying low (the lower that your eyes are to the ground the easier it is to 'silhouette' the area around you) he was bitten in the neck behind the right ear by a centipede; a large ten inch centipede that he had the presence of mind to cut in half with his knife. This hurt, it hurt him like hell, and all that we had in the aid kit for something like this was Benadryl, an antihistamine that we carried in our medic kit for insect bites and stings.

I called in our status, and asked that our lift bird remain on-station a little longer. By now Little LRRP was sobbing out loud, even though he was trying valiantly to remain silent.

It was my call, and I aborted the mission. Not only was our quiet compromised, but also I had no assurance that Little LRRP could recover, with no residual effects from the centipede's toxin. As it was, when we got back he was kept in the medic's field station for two days.

This then was my shortest mission, about 25 minutes on the ground, and the only time that one of my team-members was hurt. But I give credit for that to Mother Nature, who always seems to win, and not to the enemy!

**Another Mission**

This time we felt like we were out in the open. We were on a vast flat expanse that was almost plains like, except for the vegetation. Instead of the plains grasses that we were used to in the old cowboy movies, we were walking through four to five foot high grasses that concealed the terrain features and made everything look level from the air. A patch of green leafy brush to our front turned out to be the top foliage of a 25' tree growing alongside a streambed that was hidden from the air. Physically the going was fairly easy, but mentally it was spooky since you could literally move scores of people around in this brush and not be aware of them until you walked right into them!

Add to this unease the feeling that we were at the edge of nowhere, for to our north was the Marines'AO and we were at the northern limit of the Cav's area. This borderland was to be watched for infiltration routes that would take advantage of any security gaps between the two adjacent units. At night the effect was even more startling for there were no aircraft lights to be seen in the air to the north over the Marines' area. We knew by this fact alone that we had been spoiled by the 1st Cav's helicopter resources. The northern night sky just looked naked and barren to us, barring the occasional arty flare way off in the distance.

We had walked downslope for awhile and came to a stream bordered by some trees. We stopped to re-fill our canteens (always a good policy!) and my Montagnard Scout named Dish went for a little personal recon downstream. He came quietly hurrying back about 10 minutes later and was signaling for us to be quiet, more so than we normally were.

He told me that he had seen one individual at the stream and a couple more in the brush on the other side of the stream. They were all barefoot, not dressed for travel, and he had also seen some clothes hanging in the brush. Apparently this was a rest area of some sort.

The only thing that we could do was back off a couple hundred meters or so and we found a perfect high rise that gave us an unobstructed view of the rest area and still allowed us visibility all around. We set up as a team in some bushes and even began to relax some due to our relative security.

Soon the cigarettes were out, coffee was cooking, and I began to call in artillery after reporting to base. It felt perfectly normal to have a cup of cocoa while I was comfortably adjusting the artillery fire onto the target. We were done with our coffee break by the time the helicopters came out to assess for damage.

As one little LOH angrily buzzed the treetops over the target area, its covering gunbird orbited just above and behind it, just waiting for a target to appear. The pilots reported that the encampment area had been large enough for at least a platoon to utilize. They also reported seeing no bodies in the area but, the bottom half of a person was partly in a jungle hammock. All of the other dead had apparently been carried away by the time the helicopters arrived.

As we seemed to be in a beautiful spot, from our vantage point, I decided to stay the night in our camp spot and not risk meeting up with anyone in the grass. The mission would be over tomorrow, anyhow.

This incident is significant in my memories only in that this was my first confirmed kill due to artillery fire.

## Another Mission

This time the terrain seemed to be only up and down, when actually it consisted of innumerable valleys, ridges and fingers, all of them appearing to be gently sloping due to the lush brushy cover. There were clumps of trees and brush with the ever-present dark green grass giving it a crazily tilted meadowlands effect.

We had moved into a stand of trees with thick underbrush and were taking a mid-day break. We had learned that Charley never moved in the hottest part of the day, so we followed suit. After all, we were fighting according to the enemy's rules, and this rule was a good one. We never ate a full meal, but did snack and enjoy the break.

This mission I again had two Montagnard scouts, and their fieldcraft came through again for one of them heard something and alerted the rest of us. He pointed downslope and walked his fingers up, telling us he heard movement coming our way.

Sure enough, a couple minutes later I could hear the grasses rustle as a couple of somethings moved uphill, and my ATL indicated that he had movement on his side of our tree stand also. Everyone was alert, weapon at the ready, waiting for the first silhouettes to appear. And hoping like hell that they would bypass our little spot for we were not in a good position to defend against an unknown number. Granted, we had concealment but leaves and branches would not protect against bullets!

When the movement reached our level we got the shock of our lives, for they were GIs! We couldn't signal them 'cuz they did not know we were there and were probably more keyed up than we were, so all we could do was hope that they wouldn't notice us and pass on by. This area was a free-fire zone, and these GIs weren't expecting to come across any friendlies here, any more than we were.

Eventually about 35 GIs passed our spot, flowing around us on their way uphill as a river splits around a large rock in midstream. As soon as they were far enough away for me to use the radio I called our rear and reported the fuck-up, for that's precisely what it was – a lapse or breakdown in coordination at higher levels. For a line unit to be in a LRRP AO meant that either the line unit didn't get full clearance before deploying or that the HQ's did not pass along the fact that we were there. In either case, with all of the trigger-fingers at the ready, on both sides, it was a wonder that no one got hurt.

Our rear RTO's had their shit together and gave me the call signs and frequencies of the unit that had just surprised us. I called the platoon leader of the platoon that had flowed around us, and by now I began to see the humor in the situation. The least that I could do as I talked to the guy was compliment him on his unit's noise discipline, and that was a fact – for his men had moved in the quietest fashion that I had seen so far for Americans. Usually you could hear a line unit a mile away, literally, as GIs would holler out to one another, and some even played tape recorders of music. And the powers that be wondered why they kept getting ambushed!

Anyhow, this platoon leader was so pleased to be receiving a compliment while conducting an actual operation (heretofore unheard of!) that he asked me to meet him on his company's frequency and repeat the message so that his SIX (company commander) could hear it.

Of course I cooperated. And I played it up somewhat, for it was kind of fun to be talking to an officer who also thought I was one too, because of my call sign, and probably running a green-beanie team (Special Forces unit) because of the situation. By this time it had become 'fun' and I was 'playing'. But it could have been tragically worse, especially if one of the Montagnards had been spotted first, and this infantry Lt. was well aware of that fact.

**Another Mission**

Don't remember the mission, only this incident.

Sitting under the trees/bushes with SP/4 Anderson (Andy) from Redding, Calif. He was one of the most cheerful people that I'd met so far, and could always make me laugh. He became my asst team leader, as well as my bunk-mate. Blol also enjoyed his company and they got along great, as well.

We were sitting under a tree watching for whatever, and a flock of parrots, brightly-colored, like the kind that the pirates in the movies had, flew into our tree directly above us. There were 15-20 birds in all, hopping around, and I felt gratified that they picked our tree, for if anyone had seen the birds fly and then roost, they would never suspect that there was a LRRP team at the base of the parrot's tree!

Andy, however, put it into perspective. "Gawddamn! Do you know how much money is up there above us?"

No, I really hadn't given it that much thought. I was thinking that parrots, like all birds, shit continuously and they were above us!

**Another Mission**

This was a bad one. Even in my memories!

This started out as what I thought of as a strong team, as it was composed of three Americans and three Montagnards – myself, Sgt. Moran (a political science student from the U. of Chicago) as my ATL, and SP/4 Cain as my medic. Sgt. Moran had the second PRC/25 radio so he doubled as the RTO. The Yards were Sergeants Dish, Blol and Kit.

A typical area recon, with the normal last light insertion, only we were dropped into the wrong area and the priority was to move into the correct AO. We had to move in the dark in the direction of our intended AO, and I finally had to call a halt for the sake of security and commonsense. I was not really sure where we were, but I had an idea, based on the new insertion coordinates given to us by the chopper pilots.

This area was the open area at the northern border of the Cav's TAOR (Tactical Area of Responsibility) and the Marines' southern border. We had been in the area before, felt somewhat comfortable and 'at home' here, and still had about another three klicks to go to reach our intended AO to the west. We had been skirting the brushy clumps as we moved westward in the dark.

Since I was not positive about our exact location I opted to wait until morning and get a good terrain analysis to find out exactly where we were. I chose not to use arty marking flares, as there was no sense in drawing anyone else's attention to my spot, if anyone else was nearby. Instead, we burrowed into a fairly large clump of stickers and went to sleep, waiting for first light, thinking rather unkind thoughts about aviators' map-reading skills!

But a quiet night's sleep was not intended for us. About two hours after we settled in, we heard a large commotion, seemingly taking place all around us. And this spooked me, for two reasons. First, we were not in our star-circle, but each of us had burrowed into the center of the thicket and grabbed a convenient sleeping-spot, which was determined by the extent of the vegetation around him. And second, most critical, was the simple fact that since we were in the middle of a sticker-thicket, we couldn't get out. We were effectively trapped! I had followed the guidance of the Yards in that we could sleep in the stickers and would be alerted if anything happened around us, and because of the stickers nothing would casually intrude upon us. But we were stuck, nevertheless.

With voices and activity all around us, I asked Dish what was happening. My stomach went cold and heavy as he whispered back "many VC sleep here." Apparently they had the same idea that I had, that this would be a good place to spend the night, and as a result what appeared to be a platoon-sized element was setting up cooking fires and generally making themselves comfortable around the clump of stickers.

There were approximately 40 individuals all around us, and all that we could do was lay low and hope to remain undetected. I grabbed the radio's handset, and contacted the rear by breaking squelch. The RTO was a good one, and within 10 minutes he had received a fairly good sit-rep from me by asking the appropriate and pertinent Yes/No questions.

When the Brigade HQ's received the report, they had the closest firebase to me come up on my freq and ask if I wanted any arty support. Since I wasn't too sure of my location I said no. (I later found out that the infantry unit on that firebase was monitoring our frequency in anticipation of being sent to my assistance. At the very least it was good entertainment for them!)

That was undoubtedly the longest night of my short life. During the time that we were surrounded the VC practiced camp sanitation by using the sticker-bushes in the center of their camp as a toilet area. I had one individual take a crap just four feet from my head and shoulders, and my ATL, Sgt. Moran, had one VC urinate into the bushes, onto his back!

The VC were gone by first light, and the infantry unit that had been listening to the radio reports was lifted into my site just one hour later. We moved a short distance to marry-up with them, and to coordinate with their probable departure direction. We were a sorry-looking, exhausted bunch by then, due to lack of sleep and over-production of adrenaline. The rainy weather did not help any.

After leaving the QRF force, we started off, following the departed enemy. We had only gone about 800 meters when Sgt. Dish noticed a couple of signs in the trees, written in Vietnamese. He got scared when he read them (this then scared ME, for to me he was a rock) and he explained that they were VC warning signs indicating that the area was to be avoided since it was thoroughly mined and booby-trapped against the Americans when they ventured into it. I immediately called the infantry unit and told them I was coming back to their location.

By now the morale and energy of my team was non-existent and I requested an abortion of the mission and an extraction with the infantry unit. The higher-ups in the rear said no – they were excited by the previous night's incident and my discovery of a posted, mined area. They wanted the team to stay and reconnoiter for they just KNEW that something was up.

The infantry medic was a cool hand, and he checked us all out. He sent Cain back to the rear with his infantry people 'cuz he found some trench-foot fungus or some such on Cain's feet, but he felt bad that he couldn't do anything for Moran or me.

So Cain was med-evacked to the rear, we marched off to the west, and the infantry people stayed for another couple of hours just to make it look good.

For the next three days Moran and I felt guarded by three Montagnards, but it was a bitch at night since we were the only ones who could monitor the radio. Needless to say, I made sure that it turned into a true 'camping trip' in the rain and did not overextend my little team in the least!

[Admin. Note – About a month and a half later I ran into that same infantry Lt. at the shower facility at LZ Betty – he was still carrying his personal shotgun!]

# Chapter Ten

## The Missions Continue

This one proposed to be a fairly safe and quiet one for us – an observation mission at the mouth of a river valley that we were already familiar with. This was a stunning area visually that was similar to the rugged peaks and valleys that you usually saw painted on Japanese silk screens. We would be watching the area where the large river came out of the highlands to the west as it flowed eastward to the sea. These riverine valleys were rugged, reaching steep vertical heights of several thousand feet above the riverbed below. They were forested over as were the mountains back home in the Pacific Northwest and were a beautiful sight, more forest than jungle. To complete the picture the open plains area began several klicks to the east.

I felt that we had pulled a 'good mission' this time for we were to be inserted at the base of a solitary hill just two klicks or two thousand meters from the mouth of the valley, climb to the top (hopefully unobserved) and just sit at the top and watch for enemy movement anywhere upriver or in the flat area around us. From our vantage point we would be able to see for miles around.

The late afternoon insertion was uneventful, and by last light we were established at the top of the hill. There were some 40 foot tall trees at the summit so we were hidden from view from below, hidden from view from the neighboring ridges, and in general we were comfortably secure. There was an old military position on top, as evidenced by a series of foxholes around the military crest of the hill, and the summit was extensive enough that there was adequate space on top for a helicopter to come in and pick us up when the mission was over. Since we did not plan on climbing back down, we truly felt that this was to be a 'lazy O/P' mission.

The next day, while nosing around on top, we found four one pound blocks of C-4 explosive and two 100-round belts of M-60 machine-gun ammunition. Apparently the GIs that had been here previously were too lazy or tired to carry their loads, so they just left it in the foxholes. And the military command was wondering where the enemy got his supplies for all of his booby-traps!

On the third day of our 'vacation' we spotted six VC moving up the valley below us 1500 meters to our south. We were directed to use artillery, we were in as safe a location as one could get, we could observe our target indefinitely, so I decided to experiment.

There was a new artillery round out called the "firecracker" that everyone was excited about. Along the lines of a 'bouncing Betty', this new round supposedly started with an air burst, many little bomblets then blew down to blanket an area, bounced up and then exploded like a field of hand grenades, simultaneously. But no one had as yet tried it, so I called for it.

I had the radio in a good commo position, but could not observe the six VC as they worked the ridgelines to our south, so my ATL SP/4 Gary Anderson would give me adjustments after the initial impact round. He and Blol were on the other side of some underbrush from me to watch the show. Andy, through me, finally got the white phosphorous adjusting rounds where he wanted them and I called in fire for effect.

I couldn't see the target or the artillery barrage, but I could hear it, and it did not sound like normal HE rounds, but like a lot of little bangs occurring at the same time. I do remember Andy sticking his head over the bush, looking at me extremely wide-eyed and saying "Damn! That shit's *deadly*!" He had such a look of honest amazement and shock on his face, along with a boyish happy smile that I had to laugh.

The next humorous incident happened as we were looking through binoculars to assess the damages done to our six targets. All of a sudden Blol started laughing and whooping on the other side of the bushes. He didn't wait for me to ask, but barged right through the greenery to where I was and happily reported that they could see one VC carrying another wounded one, piggy-back fashion. They couldn't see the other four, so we waited for the choppers to make their visual assessment. They later found two discarded weapons, but no bodies.

The only other incident of note happened at the PZ as we were being extracted.

As we rushed to board the hovering helicopter, one of the men had some trouble with his balance and/or gear while trying to make it aboard. I think it was Little LRRP but I'm not sure. Anyhow, I was behind him balancing on the strut trying to shove him up and forward, and trying to ignore the impatient door-gunner. This guy popped forward like a cork out of a bottle, and I staggered backward. The pilots must have felt the change in weight, for they nosed forward and took off, leaving me there in shock. I had the radio so I quickly called our C&C ship and told them that I was still on the ground. SSG Steve Ward answered, very surprised, and 10 minutes later I was aboard his ship enroute to LZ Betty.

So for about 10 minutes there I can honestly say that I was (to our knowledge) the only American on the ground for about 15 miles in any direction.

By the way, it was during this particular mission that I had occasion to celebrate my 21st birthday!

*22 Aug '68*

*Hi,*

*Just thought a letter was in order to let you know that I'm all right and still kicking pretty hard.*

*We're still here at Quang Tri trying to help the Marines. They've finally changed their tactics and are starting to hold their own.*

*Hey! I've got an R & R to Hawaii at the end of the month. Be home on the eve. of the 30th and I'll call. If you're not home, I'll call the next night. Plan on staying with Bob [Carr] while I'm there. He's already left Nam and is home on leave now.*

*Plan on getting a bike when I get out – 900cc Harley. Will cost a good $1600, and will about wipe me out. Blood money anyhow, so no big gig.*

*Prepare yourself! Have decided to go into land surveying and highway engineering/construction when I get out. Will minor in philosophy to keep the homework interesting. Gave it a lot of thought and I couldn't stomach a 9 – 5 inside desk job. Like the outdoors too much. It's just not in me now to punch a time-clock.*

*Like the pictures? Thought I'd let you see a real war-mongerer in action. These were taken last month (26 July) as my team was boarding a chopper prior to a mission. The man sitting on the floor of the bird is Blol, my Montagnard front scout. Admire the hell out of him.*

*Had a real good 21st birthday. Celebrated in the boonies with a cup of cocoa. As a present, spotted 5 VC and called artillery on 'em and sorta ruined their day. Not quite the type of birthday I'd planned for so long.*

*Here's a list of all the gear I carried on the mission in the pictures. If you can't figure it out, have Uncle Len translate. For a 6-day mission, and as team leader, I carried*

*12 LRRP rations*
*10 qts. Water*
*1 CAR-15 with 31 magazines*

*1 M-79 grenade launcher w/26 rds.*
*1 PRC/25 radio w/short whip & spare battery*
*5 frags (grenades)*
*1 ea smoke and white phosphorous grenades*
*1 compass, map, signal mirror, & signal panel*
*1 .38 pistol w/50 rds.*
*1 survival knife*
*1 survival kit*
*1 strobe light (night signaling)*
*1 claymore mine (anti-personnel)*
*2 trip flares*
*1 ½ lbs. C-4 (explosive)*
*1 flashlight*

*And last, but not least, the all-important 6 packs of Pall-Malls. I'd swear that my pack weighs more than I do.*

*Got Barb's letter yesterday. Just can't believe that she's 5'1" already. Do like the material for her dress. Tell her I approve. Linda and I are fini. Got a classical 'Dear John' last month, and just didn't care one way or the other. Haven't cared much about anything lately. Hmmmn. Just want out of the Army. With a purple passion.*

*That's about it, really. You probably know about the offensive over here, so nothing else to write about.*

*Love,*
*Jim*

**Another Mission**

In terms of planning and preparation this was the most fouled-up mission that I can recall. The mission results seem to verify my views.

The 1st Cav was getting ready to move south – all the way south to

III Corps, to a place called Phuoc Vinh. Not many knew the destination, or even really cared. The fact was that an Airmobile division was getting ready to deploy to a new location and everyone had things to do.

We were closing out of LZ Betty to Camp Evans, and from there would move as a unit to our final destination. We all felt, and rightly so, that our field duty was over for awhile. But three days prior to our departure from LZ Betty we were given a mission alert and drew rations and ammo for a bona-fide mission, even though no one expected the mission to occur.

The day of departure to Camp Evans arrived and, typically, there was a change in our transportation status. All of our personnel would make the move, as scheduled, but there wasn't enough space available for all of our company gear. So all of the LRRPs and their weapons and packs were airlifted to Camp Evans, but the leftover equipment required somebody to accompany/guard it until it could be flown down the next day, which also happened to be the insertion date of my bogus mission. I was the ranking field LRRP so I was designated to remain with the equipment.

I had given up on the mission for several reasons. Various and sundry of our unit protocols had been broken, which all signified 'No Mission" to us. These included the lack of an aerial recon by overflight to designate LZs and PZs, the lack of a team warning order and subsequent five paragraph field order, no coordination with other units to obtain call signs, frequencies and expected locations, and the issuance of team gear pertinent to the particular mission.

So I remained overnight at LZ Betty as the only LRRP, and expected to catch a flight to Evans about noon the next day. I arrived, with all of the platoon gear at Evans about 3:00 in the afternoon the next day, and I was hungry. A jeep and our deuce and a half met me at the airfield, and I knew something was up, for I was told to let the others off-load the gear and ride in the jeep back to our area.

There my worst fears were realized, for the mission was still a go. I was tired and complained to Lt. Keldsen that the mission shouldn't happen, that nothing was normal about this. No matter. My team had packed my pack while I was talking with the Lieutenant, my ATL was given a handful of maps and the team SOI code book (Signal Operation Instructions), and we were told to catch a bird to an arty firebase for our last-minute overflight. I was so angry, frustrated, and concerned about all of these *wrong* things happening that I had tears in my eyes.

We all boarded a slick to the firebase, after I had been on the ground at Camp Evans for a total of about 45 minutes. At the firebase, I had the ATL do the coordinating at their base FDC (Fire Direction Control center) while I went on an overflight of the mission area in the only bird available – an LOH, and I had to act as the rear gunner with the M-60 on my lap to boot. As the bird was taking off, my RTO had scrounged a paper-plate of food from the unit's mermite containers and gave me a plate of spaghetti, mashed potatoes and bread (no spoon or fork). That's how the overflight was conducted.

After that, when we returned I then briefed the lift-bird's pilots as to the LZ location and its back-up, and we took off immediately since the bird had by now been refueled and we were losing daylight.

We ended up being dropped into the wrong area, again. This time we were dropped six klicks south of our intended AO. Our rear then adjusted my AO for the sake of arty H&I fire in the area. My new mission then became a trek northward, to my intended AO.

The only good thing was that we were familiar with the area, which is why I think we were sent in the first place. The intended AO was the northernmost ridgelines, just at the beginning of the large plains area, the border between the Cav and the Marines. While the Cav was gearing up to move, we were to watch the back door, so to speak. But we were dropped into the woodsy area, five to six klicks south of that.

It looked level, from the air. But under the level-appearing tops of 120' triple canopy, it was anything but! Mostly small valleys and ridges (similar to our Southern U.S. 'hollows') aligned west-east, and we were trying to move north in all this. So our line of march was all up and down, and hidden from the air. And at the bottom of these hollows we had no Commo, due to the height of these ridges. All in all, not a good spot to have something bad happen.

On our third day of cautious humping we found a large trail complex that criss-crossed both sides of the valley. We marveled that from the various trail levels on the "valley sides' the entire valley floor could be visually monitored, and of course, covered with weapons fire. Luckily for us it was abandoned, but we were more than impressed by the amount of time and effort, and manpower, that had to go into the construction of this place!

It was further fortified/defended by a series of two to three man fighting positions and foxholes dug into the valley sides, always on the uphill side of the trail systems. One small company of determined soldiers could hold this place against a battalion-sized ground assault. In one of the fighting positions we found several ammo boxes with Chinese markings, containing the Chi-com equivalent of our eighty-deuce mortar shells.

We were ordered to blow them in place, and to keep moving. No argument from us, as each man on the team only wanted to be away from there.

We finally reached our intended AO on the sixth day, of a seven-day mission. We were so glad to finally reach fairly 'level' terrain that I took a picture of it.

The next morning we were airlifted out. As I was scrambling into the chopper and twisting around to sit on the floor with my legs dangling out I felt a strong stinging pain on my inner right thigh, like I had poked myself on a sharp piece of metal on the flooring edge. I looked but couldn't find any jagged edges as we lifted out, enroute to Camp Evans.

We landed, rather chilled after the flight at altitude, at the helipad and began to walk to the company area. After a few steps I felt another sting on my leg and stopped to take off my rucksack. Then I felt another strong pain, enough to bring tears to my eyes, this time on my penis, of all places. I lowered my pants right there in front of God and everybody and found a small two inch scorpion in the crotch of my pants! He (?) had apparently crawled up my pants leg as we laid in the grass waiting for the chopper and managed to sting me as I boarded. He was chilled to inactivity during the flight and managed to vent his displeasure on me when we landed and he 'thawed out.' I was just grateful that he was running out of venom by the time of the third sting. I took a Benadryl (the only antihistamine in our medic kit) and continued on to the debriefing.

All in all, I really don't have *any* pleasant memories of Camp Evans!

*7 Oct '68*

*Uh,*

*Sorry about the paper [written on a yellow legal pad], but it's all that I could steal. Not much is happening out here, really.*

*For one thing, I've got a pretty bad case of the hips. I just found out that I have to stay in the field longer than I expected. It used to be that a man got pulled out approximately 30 days prior to going home. Now I find out that I have to keep pulling missions until 2 or 3 days prior. I no like. To tell the truth I'm getting scared and my nerves are shot. I ought to just go out and hide from now on – and say to hell with the missions.*

*To change the subject – something new has been added. I just found out that I've been promoted. I am now a staff sergeant (E-6) instead of an ordinary buck sergeant (E-5). It's about a $45 raise. I think they're trying to get me to re-enlist, seeing as how I've got about one month left in the Army. But I ain't gonna. I ain't!*

*I'm going out tomorrow, so I'd better quit and get some sleep. Catch you later.*

*Jim*

# Chapter Eleven

## Phuoc Vinh – Purpose

Here, in III Corps, with Capt. George Paccerelli as our CO our overall mission usage changed, from primarily intelligence gathering and observation (like a scout) to a more aggressive and active role in the hunter/killer concept. That is, if we had a quiet mission in a 'dry' AO we were expected to do some damage, if possible, prior to extraction.

Word had it that Paccerelli was a 'Mustang officer,' a former veteran Special Forces A- Team member with multiple combat tours of duty under his belt, which probably explained the change in mission.

This change did not sit well with me and some of the older, 'veteran' LRRPs (here veterans are signified by time in unit, or by time in country), for up to now the safety of our teams in the field was a direct result of the fact that the enemy did not know that we were there in the first place. Hence, we were able to take more chances and still remain undetected, up north in II and I Corps regions than we would be able to down here.

I felt that it was more of an individual challenge to sneak in and remain undetected in the enemy's backyard, than it was to chase a body count. After all, anyone can shoot, whether one was good or not, but... there were lots of medals to be earned this way. An illustrative example of this way of thinking was that the new guys seemed to be proudly counting their 'contacts', whereas the older guys would brag about how many missions they had 'completed', signifying that they had eluded detection.

As stated above our missions and general intent became more aggressive here in III Corps area.

In line with this, Capt. Paccerelli originated the idea, (and God only knows where he had them made), of wooden nickels with our unit designation on one side and an Indian's head on the other. The idea was that we were to leave a wooden nickel on our enemy KIAs in the field, to scare the enemy as it were, and to let him know that we were now in his backyard.

Personally, this struck me as insulting an enemy that I had by now come to respect, for he was undermanned and outgunned and faced a 'superior' technology, yet he hadn't given up. One <u>had</u> to respect this!

So we team leaders were given a handful of these tokens prior to each mission, for the purposes already mentioned. I didn't want to brag over the dead (nor, deep down, did I really want to kill anyone, and only admitted this to a select few), but in my case it became moot. For all of our insertion pilots had heard of these wooden nickels, and wanted one nickel from the team to record their "LRRP insertion missions" which the pilots were now starting to brag about among themselves. This was strong magic within the piloting fraternity.

So, on every mission now, I'd give the pilot(s) one or two tokens, and of course the door-gunner and crew chief might want one, so there went my supply!

## Rumors

The 1st Cav Div moved its HQs into Phuoc Vinh. Previously this area had been the TAOR of the Army's 1st Infantry Division, known as the Big Red One.

A paper sign was found in the concertina wire around the compound with the following message –

"Goodbye, 1st Division – It's been a pleasure playing war with you!
Hello, 1st Cavalry. Welcome to Phuoc Vinh!"

## Insults?

We had been at Phuoc Vinh for awhile, and some of us older LRRPs were still getting accommodated with what we felt were luxuries associated with 'rear duty' – for example, we now had wooden buildings with concrete floors to live in instead of tents, we had our own unit shower (with a heater for warm water) instead of a centralized shower point for the entire compound, as at LZ Betty, and we even had our own private 4-seater latrine next to the shower. The downside to all of this, like our own company area, was that we had to 'act like military professionals' to the extent that we now had daily company formations, something unthought of in the past!

We had a mortar attack one night but this was really no problem, for we now had our own sandbagged bunkers alongside each building in which to hide. Several of us, remembering previous living conditions in other locales, thought that this was really a safe way to fight a war. But during this particular barrage, we began to get nervous for we could hear the mortar rounds impacting steadily closer to us – they were 'walking' right to us, it seemed, before the last one landed right outside our company area.

After the all clear was sounded, several guys went to inspect the damage, some went back to bed, and several decided to stay in the bunker for the remainder of the night. The mortars usually hit our side of the compound since we had several aircraft berms just across from us and they were the normal targets.

But this time it was more personal, as the very last mortar round scored a hit on our latrine! Obviously, this hit a sensitive chord within a lot of us – its OK to try and kill us, even blow us up, for we'd do it to the enemy if given the chance. But just don't mess with our potty – that's more than rude and it'll piss us off!

## Poise & Composure

As mentioned above, we now had company formations, even a morning roll call formation. This was all Capt. Paccerelli's doing, and despite all the grumbling, the unit was turning around from what it had been at Camp Evans and a sense of esprit de corps, and belonging, was building among us.

We stood at formation in the company area, just outside the first platoon barracks, one morning as roll call was being taken and reported. Standing in formation, the barracks were behind us and we faced the Phuoc Vinh airstrip, with the helicopter POL (refueling point) across on the other side.

As roll was being taken we watched a flight of six Hueys fly in to the POL point from our right to our left. This early in the morning it gave us something to look at while all of our sleepy-heads were being accounted for. So we watched as the six slicks flew in at an altitude of 200' and were jockeying in position to achieve a tight trail formation.

It looked like the pilots were jerking one another around, for in this formation all pilots had to be very aware of their safety clearances fore and aft and maintain a safe separation. But the birds in the middle were either goofing off or having trouble, for their speeds kept changing, and the trail birds had to jerk around for safety's sake. Soon it was obvious that it was getting out of hand, and a couple of birds started to rise out of the formation altogether. This caused the others to 'fly flustered' and the gaps between the birds were no longer uniform. A couple appeared to be too close to each other, while another seemed off by itself.

Then it happened.

We watched in shock as one bird flew too close to the bird to its front, and to avoid a collision it seemed to stop in mid-air. This would have been fine, but the bird *behind* it apparently had no warning that it was stopping its forward progress and plowed right into it, from behind. We continued watching in horror, from across the airstrip, as both birds seemed to explode in mid-air into one gigantic ball of fire.

The Hueys were mainly composed of a lightweight magnesium alloy, which burned ferociously. We continued to watch both birds burn at an altitude of 150'-200' and plummet earthward. Both birds had disintegrated to nothing as they neared the ground, and we saw only the main engines hit the ground. The helicopters were literally consumed by the flames during the short descent of no more than ten seconds duration. We saw no bodies tumble, but we had just seen at least six to eight men die needlessly.

Roll call was finished, and we were then dismissed for breakfast, many of us praying, all of us wide-eyed and rather subdued.

### Another Mission

This was my first field mission down south. I had extended my ETS to extend my tour, and my rationale (at least to myself, at the time) was that I was going to use the Army to get my teeth fixed. So the LRRP First Sergeant agreed to let me extend six months as the Training NCO for the company, getting me out of the field. But with the move and all it took me a couple of months to see a dentist, and then he yanked out four teeth and made an appointment for a month later. So I said to hell with this run-around.

By this time I was getting squirrelly back in the rear. There were a *lot* of Mickey-Mouse rules to contend with, and I didn't like the feeling of doing nothing while guys I knew and liked kept going out on these rather dangerous camping trips. So I told Barney and anyone else who would listen that I wanted to return back to field duty.

Capt. Paccerelli knew of me, from the other veteran LRRPs, but I had never been a team leader for him. So he proposed that I go to the field as a front scout for another TL, as a refresher before he assigned me a team. Of course I jumped at the chance.

The team leader was a new Staff Sergeant, a 'shake and bake,' one of the Nescafe NCOs (instant Sergeants) from the States who was new in country. The Army had a new policy to flesh out its leadership ranks by taking outstanding candidates from basic training, and after AIT sending them to an NCO Academy where they would graduate as a Sergeant E-5, with the top 10% promoted to Staff Sergeant E-6. So a newbie could arrive in-country as an E-5 or an E-6 with less than 10 months in the Army.

Apparently the stateside NCO academy taught that leadership was using a strong command voice, and always being in control. An NCO is responsible for whatever his men did, thus he had to make sure it was done right.

The new Staff Sergeant was one of these. The fact that he graduated from the academy as an E-6 proved that he was very good at it. He was also from the South, the Deep South, with a ***strong*** southern drawl. He talked a lot, and talked loud. I got the impression that he thought he knew everything. Of course, with my quiet wait and see attitude, I did not hang around him much, even though we were the same rank. In his defense, and with the benefit of hindsight, this was probably his way of combating nervousness; remember, there were men who were in the unit ***longer*** than the new Staff Sergeant had been in the Army! Also, he was just being the NCO that the Army had trained him to be.

In any case, I went to the field with him as the team's front scout, which was logical since I was the most experienced one there. I thought of it as a get-over mission since I had no responsibility, and only had to walk point, which I normally did, anyway.

The leadership style that he was taught struck me as being bossy. This mission was a good eye-opener and reality check for me. The team members really had no idea where we were at any time, nor any inkling of our intended destinations. This TL was so busy telling directions and giving orders, trying to do a good job, that he forgot (or never realized in the first place) that he had an entire team to help out. I got the distinct impression that he was running a squad, as in the regular army, rather than leading a team, which was the LRRP way.

At night the shit hit the fan, and it's still fuzzy in my mind as to what really happened.

In our team's overnight position I was directly opposite the TL. I remember him being excited, calling in on the radio that we had movement all around us. He was telling a couple of team-members to shoot here, shoot there, but no one was shooting at any targets that *they* picked out. In all the noise I heard no movement.

The Staff Sergeant Team Leader threw a frag, really it was a WP (White Phosphorous) grenade, and it hit some tree branches and bounced back, closer to us than its intended target, whatever that was. It went off and started some brush fire, naturally, and this seemed to rattle him even more. In the firelight we could see, across the clearing (our intended PZ), a vertical silhouette, which could have been a human torso, but it didn't move, and I thought it was a tree stump. I felt that a human would not remain exposed like that. But the TL saw it and had me throw a frag at it, so I did.

When the extraction bird arrived the pilot was overly cautious (here read gutless) and refused to try to land in the small clearing to pick us up. He was afraid of a rotor-strike in the tiny clearing, with good reason.

SSG Barnes was the NCOIC aboard the extraction ship and stuck his head out of the chopper to look at the clearing. He then pulled his .45 pistol out of his holster, held it to the pilot's head and told him that there was plenty of room, and to land quickly.

The bird seemed to take forever to hover down, with both crewmen leaning out to watch for unseen branches. It was rather confined, and the pilot had reason to be concerned, but we didn't know any of this until after the de-briefing. We were just waiting forever down below for the bird to reach us. The helicopter was extremely exposed and vulnerable during its slow descent, but it never took any fire. Indeed, I never heard any firing, other than our own, throughout the entire ordeal.

I was de-briefed solo, separate from the team, by SSG Barnes and Capt. Paccerelli. I honestly told them both that I never felt we were in danger, that I never heard any hostile fire, never saw anything, and that I really felt that I wasted a frag on a tree stump, for reasons already mentioned.

The next day I was given a team of my own, in my old first platoon, and its call sign was 32. The new Staff Sergeant shortly discovered that being in charge of an infantry squad was different than leading a LRRP team and became a damn good team leader, even if I thought that he talked too much.

When I heard about Barney pulling a pistol on the pilot I jokingly told him that now we were even - for the ass chewing I received at Bong Son for getting his team out that night. He just laughed.

# Chapter Twelve

## Body Mission

Another mission, this time with two rookies. I let Sgt. Robert Ramos get them squared away and briefed on our team's procedures while I took care of the op-order and planning details. Going to the field with 2 new guys was not the usual way we had operated in the past, but things were different here down south. Besides, I also had Chambers and Pfc. Lewis Davidson on the team to make up for the new guys' lack of experience. I had decided to make one of the FNGs named Phillip Bailey the RTO, and the other, named Bruce Judkins, the rear scout. This way Ramos, Chambers and Davidson (my ATL, Medic and Front scout, respectively) would all be in a position to both cover and teach the newbies. Just the same, I knew I'd still catch some flack from Davidson out in the field, for I was one of the few team leaders that preferred to walk his own point. Due to my experience I just felt safer this way, yet Davidson still hated walking second in file behind me. He didn't realize it yet but he was one of the few men that I trusted to spell me by walking point for awhile.

This was to be a stay-behind mission, with our AO only 1 klick from the Cambodian border. Our Intel reported that the 9th NVA Division was staging in the safety of Cambodia, where the US Army couldn't pursue or attack them, and crossing into Tay Ninh Province to wreak havoc with the local populace. Our mission was to determine if our AO was an access route used by them.

The initial plan was for our team to go in on a combat assault with a line company and remain behind, hidden, when they were lifted out. Deceptively simple, on the surface, for I had to coordinate with both the line company commander, his artillery support group, and the lift-ship operations center as to the placement of my team during the assault. It was decided that there would be one LRRP on each empty lift bird when they picked up the line company, wearing regular GI fatigues over our normal Tiger fatigues, and we would re-form as a team in the heavy bushes on the LZ as the line company made their sweep of the area. In this fashion we would appear to be, to anyone watching the operation, as normal GIs coming in, and would not re-appear for a couple of hours after the line unit had left and it was quiet in our AO. Such was the plan.

So, early in the morning our team flew out to the 1st Brigade HQs at Tay Ninh, checked in and flew out again to LZ Tracey where we awaited the arrival of the lift ships and the line company. I re-coordinated with the artillery battery on Tracey and we had a couple of hours to eat lunch and wait. I'll be damned if Judkins and a couple of the others didn't end up shooting the breeze with a couple of Red Cross donut dollies who also happened to be on the LZ.

When we were told that the birds were in-bound I told everyone to put on their war paint (camouflage sticks were used for this) and pull on their jungle fatigues over their Tigers. This made it unbearably hot for awhile, but we knew we'd cool off in the helicopters at altitude. Each of us formed up with an infantry squad and then boarded the slicks and lifted off. As we took off and left Tracey we could hear the 105s on Tracey begin their long-distance artillery-prep of the intended LZ. I groaned in my stomach, for I knew that when we landed there would be grassfires, smoke and noise all around – not the quiet and sneaky insertion that we were used to performing.

And it got worse. As we came in on final to the already pounded LZ the door gunners on all the birds opened up with their M-60 machine-guns, and the escort ships began firing their rockets at any likely target or area on the ground. Ostensibly this was to keep the heads down of any enemy on the ground, but to us it seemed like a huge waste of armament.

We landed, somewhat anti-climactically, in the midst of all this noise and confusion, re-assembled as a team and made our way to a clump of trees and bushes adjacent to an irrigation ditch, where we tried to remain concealed as the ringing in our ears died down. As soon as I could, I contacted the line unit on the radio, told them exactly where we were, and then we waited for them to finish and leave.

For the next hour, we listened to GIs clomp around everywhere in the open, but avoiding our location, as planned. When the lift birds finally came in to retrieve the line unit, the uproar started again, for it seemed the ARA ships had had time to re-arm and brought back several LOHs with them this time. As the last of the lift birds took off the ARA ships fired rockets at the surrounding tree lines while the LOHs used their mini-guns on everything that the rockets had missed. And in all of this firing, they probably hadn't hit anything except trees, bushes and grass for the line unit had reported the area as clear of all hostiles.

After the Line Company left, we fixed dinner and ate, killing time. When a couple of hours had passed and our area became quiet again, to the point where birds and insects were making their natural noises again, we started to move out.

It was apparently an old rice-growing area, gone stagnant from disuse. We were walking in calf-deep water with waist high wild grass growing everywhere. I had my objective already selected – the corner of a tree-square that faced across the open space to the border yet it afforded a view of the surrounding tree squares. It was also on a raised dike that looked to be dry, and had trees and bushes for our concealment. It looked to be perfect for our first overnight location, so we started off.

But the area was wet, even though the vegetation appeared to be dry. These old rice paddies contained water well, and no one was around to drain them – it was like walking in a wet peat bog. We also had to cross another irrigation ditch that was waist/chest deep in water – *we're going to have to check for leeches later*, I thought to myself.

As we reached our destination I was not overly surprised that we weren't the first to realize its potential, for there were several foxholes, four feet deep, that had obviously been around for awhile. Just the same, we settled in, established a radio-check and began to make our evening coffee and cocoa. We heard some out-going mortars in the distance, and I had Bailey call it in to the rear, just to be safe (and to give him some practice.)

Then Davidson came vaulting back into the team's area with an excited look on his face and reported that he had seen six NVA coming across the open area, directly towards our position. I moved with him about seven feet to the edge of the bush that we were behind to take a look. Sure enough, about 200 meters out were six torsos, half-concealed in the grass, weaving and zig-zagging, but working their way to us. "Hey, these guys are good," I remarked. "They're not moving in a group, or making an easy target of themselves. Probably one of their recon elements, coming to see what all the fuss by the line unit was about."

We crawled back to the team, and I had everybody put their web-gear back on. "Company's coming" I said. "Let's get ready for 'em."

At this point Davidson spooked me, for he now said that they had disappeared. They were no longer in sight. It was like they were never there.

Thinking that they had made our position and me not knowing where exactly they were, there was only one sensible course of action at this point – I had Bailey call in the sighting and requested that the rear send out the Blues. With the odds even at six to six, and two of my guys brand-new, it was time to call in the infantry back-up that was on standby whenever we had a team in the field. Besides, they apparently knew where we were but we didn't know precisely where they were, except close. As to the mission, hadn't we already found out that they were coming across from the border, right over there?

With Bailey requesting the Blues on our home freq. I used my radio to contact the arty unit at Tracey. I had just established contact when I saw all six of the NVA in front of us, about 20 meters out. This time they were on line and just starting to split into two man groups, one going left, one going right, and the third coming straight forward, in our direction. I pulled a frag from my web-gear and told everyone not to fire until it detonated. Pulling the pin I counted to two and threw it front center, and high, at the NVA. I was hoping for an air-burst, or if it landed in front first, all six of the enemy soldiers would be in the killing radius of the grenade.

But nothing happened – it was a dud!

Rattled now, I grabbed two more grenades and threw them to their front as fast as I could. When they exploded we all opened up with our rifles. Of course, after our first volley we couldn't see them for they had gone to ground in the high grass. Dusk was falling and it was getting harder to make out silhouettes in the darkening gloom. While Bailey was talking to our rear and keeping them abreast of developments, I called for arty flares from LZ Tracey with my radio.

It was then that both Ramos and Bailey saw one NVA to our left front, running. Bailey threw a frag at him, and Ramos yelled out that no one could sail through the air like that and live. He had to be dead.

Things were getting dicey now, so I went over to Bailey and said, "You protect that radio. Don't worry about shooting. Put that radio in a foxhole and protect it." He, (AND the radio), was in the foxhole before I finished talking. I had to chuckle to myself in spite of it all – he was going to work out well with this team!

Meanwhile I was directing a steady flow of artillery flares, and at the same time we were shooting at any sound we heard, anywhere around us. It was downright creepy, for they had not fired back, at all, but it sounded like they were all around us in a 270-degree arc to our front.

I moved alongside Judkins, the other rookie, and told him to start peppering the open area with his M-79 grenade launcher, the closest thing to a mortar that we had. "Put a couple of rounds out about 125 meters and start working them in," I instructed.

Understandably, he was somewhat nervous, but holding up well.

He loaded the chunker, pointed it towards the grassy area, and fired. We waited for the explosion. And waited. And waited. Finally we heard a muffled whoomp! Way off in the distance, about two miles into Cambodia, it sounded like.

"You might want to bring the next round down a bit," I suggested. He took a deep swallow and fired again. This time we heard an explosion much closer, about 150 meters out. "There you go," I said, clapping him on his shoulder. "I'm not sure exactly where they are, so just pepper the area to our front, then fire at any strange sounds you might hear."

Bailey hollered out at this time that the Blues were two minutes out. Looking to the east we could see the lights of about 14 helicopters moving in our direction but way up there, to avoid the path of the artillery flares.

Bailey hollered that Talon Six (Capt. Paccerelli) wanted a sit-rep. I had Bailey reply that we had engaged six NVA approaching our position with the results of one probable KIA and two probable WIA. The other three were unaccounted for and due to the situation (it was my call) – that I had requested the Blues and wanted an extraction ASAP. Bailey reported all this over the radio as the rest of us kept firing at sounds in the brush and vegetation all around us. By now we had all of us realized, with the events of the day and this present contact in progress, that these sounds we were hearing could not possibly be wild animals. Trouble was, to my mind anyhow, these were the sounds of more than just three. How many more were out there that we hadn't seen, and why weren't they firing back?

By now the Blues were circling on station about two klicks to the North West of us. Allowing for at least two ARA ships as escort, that meant 12 birds full of infantry were orbiting up above and watching the light show provided by all of the firing on the ground. Why in the hell weren't they coming in?

Concerned now, I reached for my radio and spun the freq dial to our home freq. I picked up the tail end of an exchange between Capt. Paccerelli and the 1st Brigade Commander –

"Just how could your men be in contact in an area that had been cleared by an entire line co. just this afternoon, and they found nothing? Have them retrieve a body to verify their contact, before I'll authorize the QRF force to land."

My breathing stopped when I realized the import of what I had just overheard. Bailey was next to Ramos, his back to the foxhole, so he hadn't heard the conversation. Just as well, I thought.

Then Talon Six called Talon 3-2 (me), and asked for a current sit-rep. I repeated the previous one, adding that we were expending our ammo at sounds all around us, like more than the original six, and again requested extraction.

"Negative extraction," he said. "Search for and retrieve the KIA prior to extraction," came over the radio.

"Negative on the search," I retorted. "Too dangerous, and I've got two rookies out here. My call is for extraction ASAP."

"Negative extraction," he repeated. "Find a body or you'll lose a stripe," I heard over the handset. By this time the rest of the team was monitoring this on Bailey's radio. I couldn't believe what I had heard; especially from our CO, who himself knew firsthand just how dangerous it was out here, and also our rule that the man on the ground was in charge. Regardless!

Then I got hot. And I blew. I picked up the handset and yelled into it "I'd rather be a live E-5 than a dead E-6. And you have to come out here and get me in order to get that stripe." As soon as I said that I almost felt apologetic, for no one ever argued with Capt. Paccerelli – he was the best thing that had ever happened to our unit, and we'd all follow his lead anywhere.

"At ease, 3-2," he said in that tone that only he could use. "No body – no extraction. Find one. Fast. Out."

Deep down, I knew that he was right. Way, way, <u>deep</u> down. But still…

"Spanky, that's crazy" protested Ramos. "We can't go out there," pointing to the grass.

"I know, but it's the only way we'll get a ride home. Will you go with me?" I asked him, because it was too idiotic to order him to.

"Are you really going?" he asked with a worried look.

I nodded.

He shook his head and took a deep breath. "Yeah, I'll go."

This won't take long, I hoped, as Ramos and I worked our way to where he had seen Bailey's NVA go sailing through the air. By now the arty had stopped providing us with flares, so we were using flashlights, in waist-high grass, surrounded by guys who wanted to hurt us, just to find a body so that we could prove that we were telling the truth about being in contact. I was so angry that my clenched jaws hurt. Ramos and I looked far and wide, deep and close, and couldn't find a thing, not even a weapon. Our flashlights were too feeble to ID a blood trail even if we were looking at it.

Then a sense of sanity returned, and I knew it was wrong for Ramos and I, the ATL and TL, to be out here together, so I sent him back to the team and told him to send Davidson out to me. Meanwhile I would work my way over to where we had first seen the six enemy soldiers, on-line.

Ramos left, and I started moving. I heard some movement in a dry irrigation ditch so I threw two frags, one towards each end, and after they blew I jumped in and fired a magazine the long distance of the ditch. "OK here!" I hollered back to the team. "Just clearing the ditch." I sure as hell didn't have to worry about being quiet anymore – anybody around the area knew where I was by now.

Davidson joined up with me moments later, and we began our search all over again. If nothing else – I thought – we're giving the Blues quite a show down here.

We covered quite a bit of ground, and turned to look at the team's position. From out here it seemed like a damned good position to be in, and we turned around again.

"Davidson, look," I pointed. Off to our front about 15 feet was a huge swarm of mosquitoes. "Why are they clustered there, and nowhere else?"

We went nearer to look, and found out. There, his side ripped open by one of the earlier frags, was the body that we needed. It was all the exposed blood that had attracted the mosquitoes.

We yelled to the team that we'd found a body, and I started forward.

"Wait a minute, Spank," warned Davidson. "Booby – trap?"

Ever the cautious one, he was right. His buddies had had plenty of time to booby-trap the body if they had wanted to, so I used my rappel-seat rope to loop one of his ankles, very gingerly, and drag him 10 feet to dislodge any unwanted surprises. Nothing happened.

Then my sixth sense, what I called my combat-antennae, kicked on. "Davidson, go back to the team and have everyone come out here quietly. Whoever's around us knows exactly where our position is. It's time to move." He hustled off while I watched the orbiting Blues, looked at the beautiful natural stars filling the sky, and listened for anything and everything while waiting for the team to re-join me.

Five minutes later I heard the grass rustle and heard a worried whisper, "Spank?"

"Here!" I answered as Ramos led the group out to me.

We clustered around the body as we called back to the rear and again requested extraction. I asked Ramos if they brought everything. Everything except a bunch of empty magazines, he answered, that were scattered all around the site. We could get more back home.

While talking to the extraction ship that had finally received authorization to come in, we heard a loud metallic clattering back at our old position. Someone had walked there and stepped on a bunch of the empty magazines! As one we all opened up and blasted the be-jesus out of our old position.

The lift-bird asked what all of the fireworks were, somewhat worriedly. I replied over the radio that we were making sure that the area was secure and to come on in. He seemed to approve of that answer and one minute later Judkins was signaling him in to us with his strobe light through the barrel of his M-79 chunker. The bird landed, we boarded with our load, and the bird took off.

It was a quiet ride, nobody saying much, but thinking a lot.

We landed at Tay Ninh, and a jeep with a driver and a Major from Alpha (Apache) Troop, the 1st of the 9th, our sister unit and where the Blues came from, met us at the heli-pad. He asked who the team-leader was and I raised my hand, not trusting my voice. He told me to load the body into the back of the jeep, and while they refueled the chopper, we'd deliver it.

I had no idea where I was, but he had the driver go to the 1st Brigade TOC. We pulled up within 15 feet of two armed sentries at the doorway, and dumped the body onto the lawn. "They wanted a body so bad, well, now they got one," he said. I asked the Major if the guy who ordered me to bring back a body was in that building. He started to say something and then he looked at my face, and probably noticed the look in my eye. "Talon 3-2, or whoever you are, I'm giving you a direct order to stay in this jeep. Driver, back to the heli-pad. NOW!"

Because at that precise moment I had every intention of going inside and increase my body count by one, and to hell with the consequences!

When we arrived back at the heli-pad the Major had a quick chat with the pilots, and directed the team back onto the now refueled chopper. We lifted off again, this time heading all the way back to Phuoc Vinh.

We landed at the 1st of the 9th control pad (usually reserved for VIP flights) at about 2 AM. The CO of the 1st of the 9th, a full colonel and one of the tallest men I had ever seen, was waiting there as we stiffly made our way off the chopper. Apparently a lot of people had already heard about our mission.

He walked up to us and asked who the team leader was. Again I raised my hand, and he walked over to me while the team formed up behind me, protectively, it felt like. He looked dead at me for a moment, then at everyone else. Finally he said, "The one thing I want to know at this moment is how much ammo you have left."

That surprised me, and also got me to wondering, for I wasn't sure what we had left, either.

So, there, on the heli-pad in front of the colonel, all of us went through our web-gear and packs, and took a count. As a six man team all that we had left was zero hand grenades, no claymores, no flares, two M-79 rounds, one trip-flare, my .38 pistol with five rounds, and I had three rounds left in my rifle's magazine. Bailey had six rounds, and the rest of the team couldn't fill one magazine with all their rounds combined. None of us had actually realized how close to naked we really were.

"I thought so." Before leaving the Colonel saluted us and said, "Good job, men!"

We watched him leave, and then picked up our gear and started off to our company area and the awaiting debriefing. There would be a lot to sort out, here.

[Admin. Note – It was later discovered that another infantry line unit was deployed to that area two days later. They found four freshly dug graves in the vicinity of the action site, and our unit was given official credit for five kills on that mission. But I'll never know why they never shot back.]

# Chapter Thirteen

**Negative Morale (Actually, *Loss* of Morale!)**

Because it happened slowly, gradually and relentlessly I'm not really sure as to *when* it happened, but I do know that I was losing/had lost faith in the moral purpose of the war effort and just seemed to be going through the motions. Two years earlier I came to Viet Nam enthused, believing that we were the good guys, performing an ethically pure action for the betterment and assistance of the Vietnamese nation. But eventually moral fatigue (for lack of a better term) set in and I felt as if all of the military actions were essentially pointless and became self-serving in their own right, with no regard for either politics or the individual Vietnamese civilian, the supposed recipient of all of our efforts.

It did not happen all at once, the result of a distinct, discrete and finite event or occurrence, but rather it was a slow erosion of my moral convictions that occurred, a malaise deep inside my conscience that kept repeating, through my intimate 'inner voice', that *nothing* mattered, *nothing mattered at all,* in the long run. As I've said, I don't know exactly when this happened, but I do associate this with Phuoc Vinh, in my memories. At least I became aware of, and identified, this mental shift during my stay in the geographic locale of Phuoc Vinh.

In view of this inadequate description of my moral despondency, one significant memory stands out, among all of the other personally depressing ones, as being very indicative of my loss of faith in my leaders and is a damn good example of my confused, yet heartfelt, disillusionment.

It was while we were still up at LZ Betty that I received a letter from my on-again off-again girlfriend back home. Another typical letter, but at the very end was a startling note –

'P.S. Joe Reynolds. Did you know him? He was killed in Viet Nam last week.'

I was struck by the indifferent and casual remark, at the tail end of a letter like this. At first it struck me as being a slight to Joe's memory, but I rationalized it by telling myself that this girlfriend did not know Joe, and that I was overly sensitive since I was in Viet Nam. Joe and I were in the same high school class, were on the football team together, but did not pal around much, as high school kids seem to flit around from group to group.

Yes, I knew him, and even ran into him when we were both home on leave – he was trained as a mortarman and felt bad for me when he heard that I was trained as a radioman. The radio antenna on my pack would make me a prime target in a firefight, he felt.

Regardless, I then started a reading campaign of the weekly *Pacific Stars and Stripes*, the service newspaper, for mention of his name in the weekly casualty lists. Morbid, I know, but for some reason I wanted to see his name. But I never did, and figured that I missed it (an insult to him), or else my girlfriend had mentioned the wrong guy.

I know we took some missions after I received that particular letter, for he was in my thoughts a lot. And the move down south to the Phuoc Vinh region took some time also.

I do know that we had been at Phuoc Vinh for at least a month and a half when I came across his name in the casualty lists, reported as having been killed last week! This was now at least two months after I had received my girlfriend's letter and original notification of Joe's death overseas.

To say the least, I was stunned to finally see his name, and could only ask myself what the hell is going on here? The withholding of his name and a false 'date of death' to make the weekly casualty lists appear fewer? My cynicism and distrust seemed, in retrospect, to be continuous from this point on. Or, *if you weren't in my unit then you didn't exist, or were of no consequence*, in my worldview.

## P.O.W.

Another typical military screw-up. We were getting used to these by now, but it didn't make it any easier coping with them. We had left Phuoc Vinh by chopper in the morning and flew all the way to LZ Tracey to get ready for our stay-behind insertion. When we arrived at Tracey I was informed that the original mission had been scrubbed and that we were going into a different AO entirely – fortunately it was still on our map sheets -that in itself was a minor blessing. Still I had to coordinate new unit frequencies and locations and get this info passed out to the team in a hasty new op-order. They took it in stride – it was my problem, but they'd follow me. It was that kind of a team.

The mission concept remained the same – another stay-behind. We would be flown in wearing regular fatigues to a field LZ currently occupied by B Co, 1st of the 8th Cav. We'd fly in a regularly scheduled chow bird, mix into the unit, change into our tiger fatigues and when the unit was lifted out later in the day we would remain behind. This new AO was one and a half klicks from the Cambodian border, and we were to watch for any NVA cross-border infiltration.

We were inserted at lunchtime and made our way to the HQs group. From the air we could see that we were in a series of tree squares reminiscent of the French hedgerows of WWII. That was understandable – this was an old plantation complex left over from the French occupation. Our tree square was also being used as the company trash pit, aid station, and mortar pit. They were spending some time zeroing their mortars and having a mail call of various squad leaders at the HQs group.

We spent about an hour bullshitting with various GIs and exploring the tree square and looking at the other tree squares around us – a series of seven or eight squares, each at least 200 meters away. These squares had housed the buildings and the in-between areas were originally devoted to rice production. Now they were just overgrown grasslands.

Finally the line company airlifted out and we were alone. I had decided to wait about an hour and then move to another adjacent tree square, both to observe this one and the open area towards the direction of the border. PFC Davidson and I had already found a handful of discarded but usable C-rations that the GIs had left in their trash pit. It was common knowledge, in our unit at least, that you could always find some kind of food in old GI positions. If we knew that, the enemy did, too. That's why I wanted to keep an eye on this tree square.

But it was not to be. At least, it didn't work out that way. About 45 minutes after the unit had left Davidson spotted two individuals approaching our square across the open area. The team was already positioned in the hedgerow on the side that they were approaching, so I opted to keep them there to observe while I hotfooted it to the South West corner to emplace a claymore covering the entrance that they would have to use.

Davidson didn't like the idea of me going alone, but I would be quieter and faster on my own, plus the team covering the approaching two NVA ensured the success of this hasty ambush. So I scrambled down the tree line to the entranceway and crawled a couple of feet into the thick trunks and root works and began setting up the claymore, aiming it directly at the opening.

Just as I was jabbing the claymore's spikes into the hard dirt I heard a voice behind me, but because I was torso deep into the bushes I couldn't make out the words. *That's Davidson,* I thought to myself, *worried that I'm alone and he followed me here anyway.* I finished planting the claymore and began to back out, leaving my rifle in there as I unwound the wire spool.

"Hey, guy," I said as I pushed back to my knees and began to straighten up, still facing the bushes. "You've got to talk lower, or they'll..." was all I could utter as I finally looked at whom I was talking to. Standing six feet away from me, in the entranceway, and staring at me as if I was from another planet was an NVA, 5'5" tall, wearing khaki trousers, shirt, web gear, floppy hat and carrying an AK-47! Because my back was to him, and my tiger fatigues were not typical GI gear, he really was not too sure who I was, either. The camouflage on my face and arms further hid my identity, along with the fact that I was only as tall as he was, not your usual giant-sized American GI, by Vietnamese standards anyway.

Both of our mouths dropped open in surprise at the same time. And at this point the luck of the Irish came through for me again, for instead of shooting me as he should have, he turned his head over his left shoulder and said something to the two others behind him, the two that I hadn't noticed yet. To this day I don't know if he was warning them about me, or if he was asking them who I was. This gave me enough time to turn and jump back to my rifle, grab it, and roll onto my back, shooting the weapon between my legs in his (their) direction. In all honesty I didn't care at this point if I hit him or not - I just wanted him to go away! My rifle-fire threw their aim off, apparently, as two AKs shot the bushes above my head before all three turned and ran. I grabbed the clacker and popped the claymore, even though I was only five feet to the side. The claymore's back blast never concerned me – I had other things on my mind.

As I made my way back to the team, who were now firing at the original two still out in the open, I hollered that I was coming in. I landed in a slide just behind my teammates, as Sgt. Ramos asked me what the hell happened. I answered three more NVA surprised me, just as they popped into view in the open area, running to catch up with the other two who were nearing the tree line of the adjacent tree square.

Then it became a turkey-shoot. Out in the open waist-high grassland, 200 meters from us, were now five to seven NVA zigzagging their way to the safety of the far tree line. The six of us would shoot at one guy for a while, then switch to another target. We could take our pick – there were plenty. But it was a lot harder to shoot a running and dodging target than was depicted in all the old John Wayne war movies.

As the last of them made it into the tree line, I had Judkins use the

M-79 chunker against the tree line while Bailey, the RTO called the contact in to our rear HQs.

I had requested a gun ship to come on-station to cover us, still leery of the far tree line. Within 10 minutes an ARA ship was blasting the far tree line, while a couple of LOHs were buzzing over the grasslands.

Davidson and I went back to the entranceway to check it out. I retrieved the clacker and spare wire while he checked out the opening.

"Look, Spank," he said holding up the floppy hat he had found five feet outside the entrance. "You were shooting high." The front brim of the hat had a neat and perfect little round hole in it.

"I don't give a rip," I retorted. "Just as long as he didn't shoot me back."

We then worked our way into the grassy area, following their beaten-grass paths, covered by the remainder of the team, still in the tree line. We criss-crossed back and forth until he yelled to me that he found an AK. I started working my way to him, then noticed a pair of hands shoot straight up above the grass about 15 feet to my left. I called to Davidson to cover me as I approached, and called for the rest of the team to join us.

When the rest of the team joined us, Chambers had his medic-kit loosened up and ready to go, for I had by now yelled to them that he was shot bad in the right leg. Meanwhile Bailey was alerting the rear that we had a wounded prisoner and requested a Med-Evac. Now Chambers and Judkins began to stabilize his leg with a pressure bandage over his blown-apart knee-cap and noticed that one of the prisoner's buddies had already applied a tourniquet above his knee. He also had a minor flesh wound to his other leg.

Davidson and I looked at each other, looked at where we were, what the team was doing, and again at the far tree line. "No, we're not going over there. It's too risky. Besides, we have a higher priority," I said, nodding towards the prisoner. He seemed to have a relieved look as he understood my meaning, 'cuz he didn't want to walk across the open to that tree line either.

By now a subtle change had overtaken every one of us – our prisoner was no longer just the enemy, he had by now become our responsibility. And we were determined that he was going to make it!

As the empty slick landed to our smoke grenade, we loaded the morphined prisoner on board as gently as we could, making sure that he was in the center of the bird, surrounded by us. No chance of this one falling or jumping out, if we could help it.

The door gunner informed me that we were taking the POW all the way to Cu Chi. I just made him double-check that medical facilities would be waiting for him, since he was slipping into shock and did not really look all that good.

Strange, I thought. Just 30 minutes ago we would have killed this guy with hardly any qualms, according to the accepted rules of engagement. And I know that he would have done the same. But here we now were, pulling our poncho-halves out of our packs and trying to wrap him, to keep him warm and protected from the rush of wind from the open helicopter doors.

The ride seemed to take forever, with our prisoner getting paler every moment. But in 20 minutes, we landed at an unknown helipad in Cu Chi, where we turned him over to some American MPs escorting a field ambulance. The team took a break while the chopper was being refueled, and I was whisked away to give a mini debriefing to the local HQs. After they were done with me, we boarded the chopper again and took off for Phuoc Vinh and our real debriefing, and where the rest of our buddies were waiting. For I daresay that everyone had monitored our frequency and knew what had happened.

It was scarcely two days later that the word was going around that our prisoner had been declared an 'unarmed innocent civilian' by the intelligence interrogators back at Cu Chi. We heard this report through our RTOs, who were used to keeping their ears open for this kind of gossip and kept our base posted.

By this time I had already lost my idealistic faith in our gung-ho war effort and a political victory, and now just concentrated my efforts in bringing my teams back intact and unhurt. But this struck a moral chord within me – I felt that I could kill the enemy in a combat situation, but ethically none of us felt that we had the right, as human beings, to commit what were loosely called 'atrocities.' In effect, all of us were trying to play by the rules. After all, weren't we supposed to be the good guys, on the side of right? Also, on a base and selfish level, none of us wanted the enemy to do that to us, if the situation was reversed, so we all tried to fight what we called a clean war, if there is such a thing. In reality we were all trying to live by the warrior's code, but we weren't sure what it was, just what it was *not* – and shooting civilians was not it!

So when I heard the report concerning my 'innocent civilian' I was understandably upset and went straight to our orderly room and asked to see Capt. Paccerelli about it.

It was obvious that I was upset so Capt. Paccerelli took me into his sleeping area where we could talk in private. I explained my position to him, and did not want to be known as a team leader, or LRRP, who shot unarmed civilians. I especially did not want it on record, since I *knew* this guy was armed and would have shot me!

Capt. Paccerelli then told me that it was an erroneous report, that two prisoners were interrogated that day, and that the wrong report was originally sent out. Like he said, it boiled down to a matter of pride that I was there to argue my case, and that without pride a man was nothing.

This took me by surprise, a statement like that, from him, and then he dismissed me.

But while I was there with him I could not help but notice the Spartan conditions of his personal area – a cot, a writing desk, and his web gear hanging from the wall. But I did notice that he had two hardback books (in itself a rarity in Viet Nam) on a shelf above his cot. They were Jack London's Call of the Wild, and Dana's Two Years Before the Mast. I was familiar with both of these and was impressed that he had them.

Later, I realized that I was very fortunate to have a commanding officer that read such books, but my opinion of him, as a person and not just as an officer, changed that day. Almost to a man our unit was changing its first impression of him – from a discipline-wielding martinet in the beginning, compared to some of our previous COs, to someone who we realized genuinely cared for the unit itself. And we all grudgingly came to appreciate and respect the changes that he had made, not only within the unit but *for* the unit. Not only did I like him, but I began to admire him!

### Another Mission

Try as I might, this is all that I can recall about this mission. Not even the names of the guys on this particular mission. But, it's still amusing – the passage of time does not lessen the field humor.

We were on a break under some trees forming a sheltering canopy over our little six man clearing. The sun was out, but splintered shadows were criss-crossing our break area. And it was covered several inches deep in dry, dead rustly leaves which were ideal to sound the 'intruder alarm'. As long as we kept our movements to a minimum, for silence, it was a fairly secure break area, as such go.

I remember one man sitting; his back propped against the trunk of a tree.

All of us then heard leaves being quietly disturbed and we all went on alert.

I saw a large python body snaking through the leaves to the man's front. I chuckled to myself when I saw him pull his survival knife, for it really was a small knife compared to the bulk of the snake's coils.

Another large snake was going through the leaves to the man's right, and he got a really worried look on his face. But when a third snake revealed itself at his left front *all* of us got worried. Were we in the midst of a snake nest?

We all had our weapons now, pointed at him. Or rather, pointed at the snakes, but still in his direction. And we all intently watched this moving mass of snake humps as they passed through our little break area.

As they left us and continued on into the woods, all of us seemed to realize at the same time that it was just *one*, one ***large*** snake that we had been watching!

# Chapter Fourteen

## The Final Missions

This was the last day of the mission, and we had about four hours to wait for the scheduled extraction. We were about 150 meters from the large clearing to be used as our PZ, and we were resting under some weeping willow bushes just five meters off the main trail that we had been following/reconnoitering for the entire mission.

Again, I had two new guys on this team.

Again, a military unit had been here previously, and left a mess.

We heard noises, and eventually some NVA approached our area, scrounging what they could from all the discarded debris.

I was furthest back into the bushes, and we were essentially in the box made by the curve of the trail as it made a right-angle turn in the woods, with the clearing at the point, on the other side of the curved trail. I was facing away from the team, down the trail, while the rest of the team was facing the clearing, and up the trail.

Three NVA were working their way towards us, but the team was in a good position, in foxholes actually, and I told my ATL to hold fire until I gave the word. I wanted them to get close enough, so close that we couldn't possibly miss.

While we waited, I spotted two more NVA (that the team couldn't see) to my front, sitting on the trail. One of them was actually smoking a cigarette!

Now I began to get concerned, for I wasn't sure how many enemy there really were, and the rest of the team wasn't aware of the two that I could see.

Then all hell broke loose, and I didn't have much time to worry anymore. One of the NVA had walked to within 10 feet of the team, and they had opened up on him. I started firing through the branches at the two that I could see, about 10 meters to my front. I saw one of them roll out of my field of vision and then they were both gone from view.

When the firing stopped, about 20 seconds later, the smell of chordite was strong in the air, and our ears were ringing in the silence. But then I felt a sharp stinging at the back of my neck, then at my throat, and also at my belly.

With the gunsmoke drifting away, I had the ATL check the body to our front. Then, to the wide-eyed amazement of the two new guys, I stood up and began to quickly undress right in front of them. Off with my web-gear, then my shirt and neckerchief, and I called for Davidson to give me a hand. For I was covered with jungle ants that had been knocked out of the branches above me by the smoke and concussion of our firing.

I'm sure the two rookies thought their team leader was absolutely nuts, undressing after a hasty ambush like that, before he even had a chance to check out the enemy. But believe me, I was in a hurry for the ants were angry and taking it out on me. So there I was, half-naked in the woods, after an ambush, with another guy helping me to brush off ants, while there was a scared enemy in the woods somewhere around us, hopefully running away. And my ATL then added to the element of insanity for them, as he came back, immediately saw what was going on, and began to laugh out loud.

The end result of this ambush was one enemy KIA, and his RPG (Rocket Propelled Grenade) launcher.

My ATL pointed out to the team that they were shooting high, as all of the wounds in the enemy's body were in his head and neck. This was a good teaching lesson, as they were in foxholes at ground level, shooting upwards as he neared them. And it drove home the lesson of the gun barrel rising when fired on full automatic.

Truly, this turned into a blessing in disguise, for when the KIA's body was turned over, we discovered that he was also wearing a carry-case with three extra RPG rounds in it that could have been detonated by our high-velocity bullets. But not a wound to his chest, to allow this.

Strange, how fate works.

### Another Mission

We were well into the mission, although I couldn't tell you what day of the mission it was.

I am on point and we are moving through the woods, with Davidson directly behind me. I'm using an animal trail through the brush, a virtual tunnel through the undergrowth, as this is much safer to follow than a man-made trail.

I turn a bend in the path, freeze, go down onto one knee and point my CAR-15 straight ahead. That's all that Davidson, immediately behind me, could see and he gave the warning to the rest of the team.

I keep my eyes forward, motion Davidson to me and he creeps silently to my shoulder and peers around the corner to my front and he sees the same thing that I do....

The brush is thicker and denser up ahead and the animal path is truly a tunnel, about six to seven feet high, and nearly four feet to our front the entire pathway, barring an opening about one foot high from the ground is enmeshed by one *gigantic spider web*! And high in the middle of the web sits the largest spider that I have ever seen - about 24 inches from top to bottom, and evil-looking. I have no idea what kinds of insects it fed on, but the monster's web looked like it could have easily snared small birds as the spider-web strands appeared to be of the same diameter as small soda straws. It was a hellish, macabre vision to see – and the startle effect was off the charts!

Davidson froze, the same reaction I had. Neither of us had moved, and the rest of the team succumbed to curiosity and began to crowd around the corner. They pretty much had the same reaction. We were ready for anything, we thought, but this was beyond the pale. Nobody could have been expecting this, in a combat situation. We were all spooked, that's the only word that fits. We were prepared for all kinds of human surprises and booby-traps; but not this! Speaking for myself, I almost shot the damn thing.

After we all stared at it and studied it for a few minutes, and regained our composure, the false bravado in the kid within all of us surfaced and someone got the bright idea of spraying it with insect repellent.

There we were: a combat LRRP team, acting like children and giggling low as we all sprayed a stream of bug juice directly at it.

But it had no effect – none, whatsoever! Three or four streams of liquid bug repellent, which worked against Viet Nam's notorious mosquitoes, had no effect at all. The damn thing stayed there, unperturbed, in mid-center of its web, as juice dripped from it onto the trail below the web.

Then I *really* got spooked, and said out loud what I knew everyone was thinking

"What if this thing is also a jumper?"

We got the hell out of there, and left it alone, still dripping.

I'm not ashamed to say that I know I would have lost all control, completely, if that thing had jumped in my direction.

To this day, in my mind, this remains 'the spider mission.'

### Another Mission

This one was up in the Song Be area, way to the northeast of Phuoc Vinh. I think it was an area recon for the 3rd Brigade. Really don't remember.

We were in a double-canopy section of forest, with many good-sized clearings scattered about so that the feeling of a large continuous forest never really seemed to sink in on us. The trees topped out at about 90 feet in height for the tallest of them, with a less dense underbrush than we were used to up north. Just the same, the filtered sunlight we encountered at ground level, plus the stark 'flatness' of this southern terrain made the woods seem spooky. The feeling of unease never seemed to go away.

We had been moving for a couple of hours, skirting clearings and trying to stay in the forested patches, encountering various trails that were unmapped. We were trying to establish, vis-à-vis the map, which trails were new and which were older and unused. Trying to find movement routes that were unobservable from the air, actually. And anything else that we found in the AO that just didn't seem right, we investigated.

We were now violating a cardinal rule of the unit – never walk on trails. But this one was too good to pass up: it was what the military called a hi-speed trail that was *very* well used. It had a hard packed dirt surface, with no vegetation growing on it, indicating frequent use, and well defined edges. It was not on the map and I wanted to find the extent of it. This info the Army could use.

I rationalized my actions this way: we had passed a clearing good enough for an emergency PZ at the beginning of the trail, and it was close enough to noon that nobody but us should be up and about. We were now about 300 meters from the clearing, and for the past 75 meters I was getting increasingly unnerved by all of the fresh signs – candy wrappers and cigarette butts were growing more plentiful on the trail the further into the woods, and the farther from the clearing, we went. This trail had clearly been used by lots of people, people who were confident enough to smoke and eat candy on it, indicating that they felt secure and relaxed here. And from the crinkliness of some of the wrappers and fresh-looking appearance of some of the cigarette butts, it had been used just recently.

Finally, I couldn't take it any longer My combat antenna, my survival sense, kicked in and shouted to my consciousness in no uncertain terms *"We are in the wrong place!"* So right there, standing in the trail, I turned around and motioned to the entire team to about-face and backtrack. And in a hurry.

It seemed to take only a minute and we were about 25 meters from the clearing, and the beginning of the trail. Everyone knew by now that I had had a bad feeling; and they all knew, from past missions, that my hunches/feelings were usually right.

I had the team just fade into the brush off the trail, opposite the clearing side, and told them to catch their breath while I set up the 12-foot jungle antenna in preparation for a Commo check with the rear. We were not in a true team position, rather everyone just plopped into the brush where they could find a spot, and we were only about 8 feet from the trail. I was propped against a tree stump that supported my pack and kept the antenna upright, but I could not see the trail, just a couple of the team members who could view the trail.

I swear, that as I was trying to establish Commo with our base, we all heard chattering and clanking from the direction from which we had just come. As we all tried to sink lower into the bushes, I had the presence of mind to loudly whisper to the team not to shoot. If the enemy felt safe enough to smoke on this trail, they probably wouldn't be looking for any trouble to find them. And if they were not looking *for* us, they probably would not *see* us. The enemy was just as blind in the jungle as we were. And if we kept our cool and remained motionless we would be virtually invisible to them, as low in the foliage as we were. Or so I hoped. In any case, we were not ready for a shooting contact!

No sooner had I reported that I had NVA on the trail, then they started to pass by us, at a good pace, in a hurry. I froze with the handset against my ear to muffle the static noise, and heard our base ask how many there were. I wasn't facing the trail, so I had a guy named Roberts give me a finger-count as they passed by, and I broke squelch once for each individual that he signaled.

I was breaking squelch for about the fifteenth time when I saw PFC Davidson, and my heart sank, for he was laying against his pack facing the trail, within 6 feet of it, actually, and he had his hat off! Ordinarily, this was no problem, as I didn't wear a hat at all, but he had the brightest, yellowest blond hair of anyone in the unit. And it stood out in a glaring contrast to the browns and greens that we trying to hide in. It was now out of our hands, as to whether we would be spotted or not.

For the next few minutes all I could do was break squelch as a total of 64 well-armed and well-equipped enemy trotted past within six feet of us, carrying mortars, machine-guns, and ropes. And they never did spot us, even though I later found out that one of them looked directly at Chambers, holding his grease-gun dead on the NVA, but he couldn't believe what he was seeing, so he kept on going.

After they were gone, and I again could talk on the radio, some choppers were sent out to check the area, and pick us up. They found footprints at the nearby river where they crossed, but not the enemy themselves.

Again, my guardian angel added to his ulcer!

### Another Mission

Disgust and bile still well up within me whenever I recall this one – to me it signifies the limits of inner helpless frustration and ineffective unfocused anger.

This started off as an area recon, in the same vicinity as the mission where I got the POW, and only about two weeks later. This required a long flight from Phuoc Vinh to another distant LZ, from which we would stage for the final insertion. I did not like the distances involved because the longer that we made the chain of involvement between my team and our rear HQs, the more apt were we to discover a weak or broken link. I had previously learned about Murphy's Law the hard way!

We also had to make a stop at some out of the way artillery base so I could do some final coordination prior to insertion, and this is where things started to go sour. It struck me as some podunk LZ alongside a civilian highway in extremely flat terrain. This really had no good feel to it in the security sense, plus it was dry and very dusty – just not a good place for artillery to be.

I had to coordinate with a pompous, arrogant and self-important First Lieutenant, who happened to be the battery commander, the artillery CO. While sitting in his office in a sandbagged bunker, dug down into the ground like a lair, or trap (I felt), it seemed to me that he was going out of his way to make me realize just how dangerous my proposed mission would be. He kept referring to the distances involved, the time for a QRF to be of any use to me, and how isolated *his* LZ was. I really got the impression that he was trying to scare or intimidate me, and this all started when he got a good look at me in person – my baby-face had caused some problems before, and I still did not have my war-paint on. He probably felt that he was wasting his time with some school-kid.

I kept my cool until he hit me with his ace in the hole – “And the area that you’re going into is not pacified. Why just a few days ago another reconnaissance team managed to capture a prisoner near your proposed AO”, he said smugly.

“I know, Sir,” I retorted. “That was me and my team that got the POW, and in this grid square,” I said as I pointed to his wall map. For the rest of our meeting, this particular officer was distinctly discombobulated and did not meet my eyes for very long, if at all.

We were inserted, without event, and spent a couple of days roaming from hedgerow square to hedgerow square in flat-ass terrain.

Then one night we were in the corner of a square, overlooking some dry growing fields. Our corner was adjacent to some trees that apparently had been planted to provide shade for the section we had chosen for our night halt. All in all a very cozy area. But then Murphy’s Law…

The majority of the team was alongside a retaining wall next to the trees, and I was several feet away on the abutting wall, with my radio and the starlight scope, checking the open area to our front. I spotted an individual about 200 meters away and coming in our direction. I alerted the team, kept him under surveillance and tried to raise our rear on the radio, but I had to go through a radio relay due to the distances involved.

The RTO on duty was not monitoring his set, as I tried in vain to raise him for a couple of minutes. By now the man that I had spotted earlier was only 60 meters to our front and looking straight ahead carefully at something that caught his attention. Through the starlight scope's green and white panorama I could make out his rifle (an AK-47), his NVA pith helmet, and his web gear. This was not a VC or a lone wanderer; this guy belonged to a unit, dressed like that, but where were they?

By this time he was too close for me to talk into the handset, so all I could do was break squelch repeatedly, to get the attention of the RTO at the relay site. But he was apparently a dud, or not very well trained, for he did respond once and asked if any station was trying to make contact with him. I broke squelch again to signify yes, but he did not pick up on this... he apparently thought some radio somewhere was randomly transmitting.

To make matters worse the NVA unit made its specific location known to us as we heard a lot commotion on the other side of the retaining wall, under the trees. It sounded like 20 to 25 individuals were gathering together, 15 feet from us, and began to make all the requisite noises, and accompanying smells, associated with a communal meal being prepared.

Great! One guy out on lookout while his unit chows down next to us, my team is about 10 feet away from me, and I can't raise anyone on the radio! Our only hope was to remain silently in place, and hope that no one from our neighboring group got up to walk around after his meal.

Meanwhile, I was still frantically trying to raise the relay station, and keep the lookout under observation. For the next hour and a half, the RTO at the relay site would periodically come on the air, but never picked up on the fact that someone was intentionally trying to raise him – he never asked the pertinent questions, and I got the feeling that he was either untrained, or not one of ours. It's a good thing, really, that I never did find out who was on duty that night. All we could do was to wait out the night, sitting there pissed, scared and angry. Eventually I got so angry that I gave up on the radio, and just kept my attention on our visitors and their lookout.

The neighboring NVA were gone by first light, and then I could pass on the events of the night by voice, and there was little doubt in either my voice or my words that I was extremely upset as to the lack of RTO support the relay station had provided overnight.

The only positive thing that I can say about this particular mission is that the enemy lookout was crouched in a clump of pineapples, and this was the first time that I had seen pineapples growing naturally!

### Another Mission

This was another area recon for the 3rd Brigade in the Song Be region, to the northeast of our home base at Phuoc Vinh. We couldn't pick and choose our missions, but nobody really liked pulling missions in this area at all. There were roads, for carts and motorized vehicles, and trails everywhere; plus, it was also a semi-populated area. Our history of primarily working in free-fire zones had definitely spoiled us in this respect, for here we would have to be sure of our targets before we could shoot.

Again, I had two new rookies that I was breaking in on this team.

It was the third day of the mission.

We had stopped for a Commo check in a relatively open area near a well-defined trail. The open area (relative to the rest of the forest) was covered in fallen logs. Whether this was the result of intentional logging or the result of past bombing we couldn't be sure – but the logs had few branches still attached – they might have been salvaged as firewood by the locals, for all we could tell. They were piled in a jumble, like jackstraws, and we wormed our way in, both for cover and concealment during the radio check, and for a safe place to observe the trails while we were there.

I ended up sitting across from one of the rookies, and we were in between two large logs. I had the radio and antenna propped against the log behind me and from where I was I could see over the rookie's head down the trail behind him. He, of course, could see past and behind me. The other team members were similarly ensconced in the log pile.

We had about one hour to go before our scheduled call-in time, and we were cooling it until then.

We had been in position for about 25 minutes, when I noticed that the rookie hadn't moved recently. In fact he was staring intently over my log to the area behind me. And his wide eyes said that he was looking at something fascinating. Wondering what could hold his attention like that I asked him what he was looking at.

His answer rattled me to no end. He said that he was "Watching three men walking up to us."

I understood that he was new in the woods, but this was ridiculous!

"Do they have packs and weapons?" I asked him, and he said that they did.

"Well, shoot them," I fairly shouted. "Shoot the bastards!"

As he started firing, I craned my head around and up for a look-see. I could see three NVA about 40 meters from us stop their approach and scurry back to the wood line. They acted as if we took them by surprise. I managed to fire two rounds from my chunker (M-79), and then fired two magazines with my CAR-15. By this time the entire team was firing as the last of them faded into the trees about 100 meters distant.

When the firing stopped, and after I had called it in to the rear, we went to check out the area. The recon birds were on their way, so this seemed like a good time to do so.

About six meters into the bushes we found a blood trail, indicating at least one of them was wounded, and we also found three 50 pound packs of rice that they were hauling. Attached to each pack were two Chi-Com hand grenades.

Later, I asked the rookie why he waited so long to tell me what he had seen, or why he didn't start shooting sooner. His answer – he was amazed and stunned because he had "never seen the enemy before, and they were so little!"

### Mission 54

Again, this was in the Tay Ninh area – flat terrain, 40 foot tall trees in a naturally woodsy area with bona fide clearings, not hedgerow tree squares in among overgrown harvest fields like the last few missions had been. And, this was a free-fire zone, with no civilians with which to contend as we stalked and stomped in the woods. Our mission, the usual area recon, looking for used, unmarked trails and any targets of opportunity.

This was the last day of a six-day mission, and we were breaking for midday, with our anticipated extraction just five hours away. Our intended PZ (Pick-up Zone) was a clearing just 400 meters up the trail complex that we had been dogging for the past couple of days.

So far we had struck out, but each of us had the antsy feeling of being watched, with the resultant itchy-skin feeling. We felt that something was *near*, just not *here*. Not yet.

We were off the trail, by 20 meters, in a good spacious opening where we could all stretch out comfortably, and still we had good security, due mainly to the thinness of the underbrush and the thick layer of dead leaves which was a contributing factor to the good visibility we enjoyed.

Again, Murphy's Law...

As we were eating lunch and really relaxing, considering the situation, we heard scuffling on the trail. We went into our drill; weapons ready, and waited.

Eventually seven NVA soldiers, without packs, hurried past our location at a good clip. There were two items of note in this sighting: first, they were in a hurry, *without* packs and second, they all wore red collar tabs, indicating they were of officer rank. Something wasn't quite right with this picture, and I voiced my concerns in my sit-rep to the rear – where were they going in a hurry without the need of packs in the jungle? They had to come from somewhere, be going somewhere else, yet secure enough in the area not to have to man-pack their own provisions.

I then exercised all of the command authority that I could muster, and convened a team meeting (it wasn't hard), and voiced my curiosity over the sighting to the rest of the team. They also shared it.

The weather was very good, we were not tired, we still had adequate water and we all felt that something was up, that we were close to something. So I then proposed an idea that had never happened before. Instead of getting shot out early from a mission, like we all had before, why don't we request to *extend* the mission 24 hours, and really check out the area up the trail from which the NVA officers had come?

I felt that the team would have to agree unanimously before I would call in the first-ever field-requested extension of a mission. We all had our E&E (Escape and Evasion) ration left, enough water, and felt good enough that one more camping day wouldn't hurt, since the terrain was mild and level and they knew that we weren't going to push it.

Everyone on the team felt as I did, and agreed to stay, plus they kinda liked the idea of being the first team to do so.

I called in the request, it got passed up through the necessary channels, and the immediate reply was that we would have to wait for verification and permission from the different artillery and aviation units that had expected us to be out by then, plus they needed time to reschedule our extraction birds.

One hour later we had our answer – the rear had approved our request. We would delay our extraction for 24 hours exactly, at the same LZ. In effect, we got another day to dawdle and nose around the area. Perfect.

After we sorted out our remaining food supplies, we had enough for a good morning breakfast, and then nothing but maybe coffee later on, but we could always get seconds back in the mess hall at the rear, tomorrow night. We gathered up our gear and started off. Up the trail approximately 300 meters, and at the edge of our intended PZ, we found a network of trails that seemed to point to a section of trees about 600 meters distant. We just knew that something was there.

It was about an hour from dusk when we pulled off the main trail, just past a Y-juncture, in preparation of alerting the rear HQs as to our exact location and intentions. I had my map-sheet spread out, and was getting the coordinates of the suspicious section of trees to call back in, when SP/4 Chambers alerted us that he heard movement on the trail behind us.

We all went on alert, more so than we were already, and three more

NVA came trotting up the trail behind us, again at a good clip. And they were headed for the targeted section of trees. The odd thing was, the middle individual of the three was wearing a white pith helmet, and not the standard tan colored issued helmet.

We were in a real good spot for a hasty ambush, so I told Chambers to keep our back trail covered, that I didn't want any surprises from behind. I slowly rose from my crouch and braced my rifle against the trunk of a tree and sighted in on the individual with the white helmet. After firing off a couple of quick bursts, all three targets had dropped to the ground as the rest of the team opened up on them, just 40 meters to our front.

When the firing stopped, I had the team pepper the area to our front with hand grenades before venturing out to check the bodies. The grasses were about four feet high here and it was too easy to walk up on a wounded enemy. Plus it was getting dark, and I was playing it cautious.

SP/4 Stan Lento stood next to me as we threw out some frags, and the second one that he threw had a double malfunction. The fuse popped as soon as he threw it, about 6 ft in the air from us, but it fizzled, rather than exploding. Good thing, too, for if it had detonated properly it would have killed us both. Stan and I looked at each other, and shared a scared smile. Then we threw another frag. One does take one's chances, in war!

The haul from this particular ambush was two enemy KIA, their weapons and their personal gear. Only one was wearing a pack. The one with the white pith helmet was later determined to be an NVA Major, and he had a folded note in his wallet with writing across the front of it that was later translated as *'Destroy if captured.'* This particular document was/were the attack plans against a nearby American firebase for the very next night. Our unit got credit for thwarting the impending attack, for it never occurred.

As to the section of trees, we were never told what was there, or if any units ever investigated it at all.

As to personal mementos of the mission, the dead Major was

carrying two certificates of achievement (their equivalent of medals) so I donated one to the unit's trophy room and kept one. I also obtained a pair of Chi-Com artillery spotter's binoculars, which I had to register in order to bring them home as an authorized war trophy.

Stan Lento chose the Major's metal canteen, which was inscribed with writing and scenery.

And the poor schmucks on that particular firebase were never attacked, at least the following night. And they never knew anything of our activities that night!

And we never did stay for an extra day on the mission, even though we were set for it!

Oh, well.

*7 May '69*

*Hi,*

*By the time you receive this letter I'll either be on my way home or will leave Viet-Nam that day. And will leave my home of the past 3 years for the final time. In a strange, unexplainable way I am going to miss this place – the good times, the bad times, the excitement, the boredom, the anger and the fear; not to mention the people. It is almost impossible to invest time and oneself in an affair without becoming involved to some extent.*

*Physically, at a casual glance, I leave here basically the same as when I first arrived – a little thinner perhaps, and my teeth worse, but in the long run none the worse for wear and tear.*

*But as a person and the complexities involved therein – a drastic change. In all truth, I personally believe that my mental age remains at 19 ½ years. Or approximately ½ year older than when I first arrived here, even 'tho I am now advancing on 22. There are a couple of solid, sound reasons for this. The first – my social life and sense of etiquette has been nil since I arrived here, and this will be a drawback when I return. Plus I will have no ability whatsoever to talk intelligently and knowingly with my own age group. They have progressed, or regressed as the case may be, as time went on in current events, etc., while I have remained at a standstill, so to speak, and regressing, in effect, by doing so.*

*Concisely, I feel myself to be inadequately prepared to blend right back into my former role as ol' Jim Seymour, a happy nothing, without some form of transitional stress. And it is precisely this stress that I fear. It will be unique and difficult, and because it is so different, I do not have the chance to prepare myself for it, and thus I am apprehensive about the whole affair.*

*And maturity. Please don't expect a world-wise young man to come striding in when I arrive. I feel I am still a young kid who never had the time to let off steam with his friends. And I believe it will be the young kid, not the young man, who will stand in your doorway. Or a cross-breed of the two, favoring the young kid.*

*So much for my seminar on "The Bleakness of Youth," and now for the newsy part of the letter.*

*Within the next 10 days I will be out of the Army, a civilian, with no more major worries than money and taxes. Twice today our captain has talked to me about staying in the service. He wants me to go to OCS and become an officer, as he did. He has already convinced himself that I should go, and now he's working on me, subtlely.*

*And I don't know if I've mentioned this before or not, but I plan on staying in Calif. for about a month before coming on home. I've got a couple of friends that I have to visit, so I'll just see 'em on the way and take my time doing it. If I don't see them while I'm actually there, I'll never get around to it. I know me.*

*Remember Joe Keshler? He's out at Bong Son with the 173rd Abn, LRRP, doing the same thing that I'm doing. We've been writing each other off and on, mostly off. Anyhow, he came down to my outfit last week to see me, and I was gone! I was out on a mission in Tay Ninh Province and didn't get back until 3 days after he left here. The one chance we get to see each other, and I blew it. I was sorta ticked off when I found out I missed him. He gets out of the Army in June, so we'll see each other back home.*

*I'd best cut this short now, so be expecting a phone call (collect) from Calif. within a couple of days of this letter.*

*'Til then,*

*Love,*
*Jim*

# Glossary

**aerial recon:** reconnaissance of a specific geographic area by means of aircraft, using either helicopter or fixed-wing

**air strike:** air-to-ground attack by fixed-wing fighter-bomber aircraft, usually jet-aircraft

**AIT:** Advanced Individual Training; specialized training taken after 'boot camp,' or Basic Training

**AK-47,** or **AK:** Soviet-bloc manufactured combat assault rifle, 7.62 mm, also called the Kalishnikov AK-47

**AO:** Area of Operations; specific location established for a military unit's planned operations

**ARA:** Aerial Rocket Artillery

**ARC Light:** a B-52 air strike

**artillery fan:** an area that can be covered by existing artillery bases

**arty:** shorthand, abbreviated term for artillery

**ARVN:** pronounced 'Arvin;' the Army of the Republic of Viet Nam

**base Camp:** known as the rear area; a location for headquarters units, artillery batteries, and airfields; a resupply area for field units

**Battalion:** a military unit comprised of a headquarters and two or more companies, batteries or similar units

**Battery:** an artillery unit, equivalent to a company

**berm:** a built-up earthen wall used for defensive purposes or protection

**break contact:** to disengage from battle with the enemy

**Brigade:** a tactical and administrative military unit composed of a headquarters and usually two or more battalions of infantry, with other supporting units

**bush:** the jungle

**C and C:** Command and Control; normally the helicopter from which the commanding officer safely commands and directs his units on the ground, far below him

**C-4:** a stable, pliable plastique explosive, white in color

**carbine:** a short-barreled, lightweight automatic or semiautomatic rifle

**CAR-15:** carbine version, with an extendable stock, of the M-16 rifle

**Chicom:** Chinese communist

**Chinook,** or **CH-47:** a dual-rotor, heavy-lift cargo helicopter used for transporting both men and equipment

**clacker:** firing device used when manually detonating a claymore mine

**claymore:** an antipersonnel mine which, when detonated, propels hundreds of small steel shot (steel bearings) in a 60-degree fan-shaped pattern to a distance of 100 meters

**commo:** shorthand for 'communications,' usually via radio, sometimes by field-telephone

**Company:** military unit consisting of a headquarters and two or more platoons, for a total of roughly 70 to 90 men

**concertina wire:** coiled barbed wire used as a defensive obstacle, normally employed on the outer perimeter of a fixed installation

**debriefing:** the gathering and gleaning of detailed information and intelligence conducted after every mission

**DMZ:** the Demilitarized Zone; the dividing line between North and South Viet Nam established in 1954 by the Geneva Convention

**double canopy:** jungle or forest where the trees create two distinct and separate layers of overhead vegetation

**E & E:** Escape and evasion; on the run to avoid pursuit and/or capture by the enemy

**elephant grass:** tropical species of tall, razor-edged grass indigenous to Viet Nam

**ETS:** Estimated time of separation from service; i.e., military discharge date

**FAC:** Forward air controller; an Air Force spotter plane that coordinates air strikes, and sometimes artillery, for ground units

**fire base:** an artillery firing position, normally guarded by an infantry company

**freq:** shorthand for radio frequency

**gunship:** an armed helicopter

**hootch:** slang for a hut or simple dwelling

**I Corps, II Corps, III Corps, IV Corps:** South Viet Nam was divided into four military regions, with I Corps being the northernmost, adjacent to the DMZ, and IV Corps the southernmost, the Delta region

**intel:** intelligence information

**klick, or K:** shorthand for kilometer (1000 meters)

**LP:** listening post; normally a two-man position set up at night, outside and forward of the unit's defensive perimeter, which acted as an early warning system in the event of attack

**M-14:** the standard-issue 7.62 mm semiautomatic/automatic rifle used by U.S. forces prior to the implementation of the M-16

**M-16:** the standard issue 5.56 mm semiautomatic/automatic rifle, with a hardened-plastic stock and hand-grip, that became prevalent in the Viet Nam conflict

**M-60:** the lightweight 7.62 mm belt-fed machinegun that was the primary automatic weapon of U.S. infantry forces

**M-79:** the individually operated, single shot 40 mm grenade launcher

**Montagnard:** the French-Vietnamese term for 'mountain people'; several tribes of indigenous peoples who lived in the mountainous highlands along the Vietnamese/Cambodian border

**NVA:** North Vietnamese Army; an infantry main-force soldier, or regular, trained in North Viet Nam and sent south to fight – easily distinguished from a VC by their uniforms, weapons, tactics, etc.

**OP:** Observation post; similar to a listening post, but the goal here is to observe for any enemy activity, rather than listen

**op order:** operations order; a plan for a mission conducted against the enemy, thoroughly covering all possible aspects of the mission

**overflight:** an aerial reconnaissance of a proposed mission area for the purpose of selecting possible insertion/extraction sites, routes of travel, water availability and prominent terrain features and landmarks. Ideally, the overflight was conducted two to three days prior to the mission not to draw undue attention of the enemy in the area, and with the same pilots to be the insertion pilots

**perimeter:** as the name implies, this is the outer boundary of any unit's ground location or site; the area outside the perimeter is unsecured

**Platoon:** an integral element of a company, usually comprised of two or more squads or sections

**point:** the forward, lead element of a unit on the move; the 'point man' is the first individual of a team, squad or platoon

**PRC-25:** the standard-issue platoon/company FM radio

**PRC-74:** a heavier longer-range radio that replaced the PRC-25

**PSP:** perforated steel planking used to build airstrips, bridge surfaces and a number of other functions

**radio relay:** a communications team or site, located in a position to relay radio traffic between two points

**Regiment:** a military unit consisting of a number of battalions, comparable to a brigade

**RPG:** a rocket-propelled grenade; a Russian-made anti-tank grenade launcher

**RTO:** radio-telephone operator; the individual soldier who carried the unit radio and was responsible for all unit communication

**sapper:** VC/NVA soldiers trained to penetrate enemy defense perimeters and, with demolition charges, destroy fighting positions, ammo and fuel depots, vehicles and aircraft, and command and communication centers

**satchel charge:** the weapon of the sapper, this is an explosive charge several times more powerful than a grenade, that is normally carried in a canvas bag across the chest and activated by a pull cord, then thrown or placed on the target

**single canopy:** jungle or forest where the trees create only one layer of overhead vegetation

**sitrep:** situation report, transmitted via radio to an element's parent unit or headquarters, to provide information and data on the reporting unit's current status and intentions

**spotter round:** usually the first round of an artillery barrage, this was normally a colored smoke or a white-phosphorous round to help the callers adjust the rounds onto the target. This was sometimes also called a **'marker round.'**

**starlight scope:** a night-vision device that acts as an image intensifier by using amplified reflected light to identify images and targets. The optical field will appear green to the observer.

***Stars and Stripes:*** U.S. military newspaper

**stay behind:** an insertion technique whereby a reconnaissance team drops out, or remains behind, as a larger unit moves on during a tactical operation

**strobe light:** a small device that employs a highly visible, and extremely bright, flashing light used to identify one's position at night. This was normally used only in extreme emergency situations.

**Tet:** Buddhist lunar New Year and the celebration of Buddha's birthday

**thumper:** slang term for the M-79 grenade launcher

**TOC:** tactical operations center, similar to the "War Rooms" of WW II

**tracer:** a round of ammunition chemically treated to glow or leave a visible smoke trail so that the gunners can accurately adjust fire onto the intended target

**triple canopy:** forest or jungle with trees of varying heights forming three distinct layers of overhead vegetation

**URC-10:** a small, two-part, pocket-sized radio that transmits either code or voice messages on UHF (ultra high frequency) used in extreme emergencies only

**VC:** Viet Cong; the irregular Communist backed guerilla forces that opposed the U.S. forces in South Vietnam

**warning order:** the formal notification, prior to an op order, given to a team in order to begin preparations for the impending mission

**WP:** white phosphorous, a fiercely burning (upon contact with the air) chemical in artillery rounds, and some grenades, that was effectively used for marker rounds. Radio slang terms included **Willy Pete** or **Wilson Pickett** rounds

# Suggested Readings

Lanning, Michael Lee. *INSIDE THE LRRPS: Rangers in Vietnam.* New York: Ivy Books, 1988

Stanton, Shelby L. *RANGERS AT WAR Combat Recon in Vietnam.* New York: Orion Books, 1992

CPSIA information can be obtained at www.ICGtesting.com
Printed in the USA
LVOW06s1341090414

380979LV00002B/419/P

9 781478 729839